The Outlook for Tokyo

New Opportunities or Long-term Decline for Japan's Financial Sector?

A Chatham House Report

Vanessa Rossi

CHATHAM HOUSE

www.chathamhouse.org.uk

Chatham House has been the home of the Royal Institute of International Affairs for over eight decades. Our mission is to be a world-leading source of independent analysis, informed debate and influential ideas on how to build a prosperous and secure world for all.

The Royal Institute of International Affairs
Chatham House
10 St James's Square
London, SW1Y 4LE
T: +44 (0) 20 7957 5700
F: +44 (0) 20 7957 5710
www.chathamhouse.org.uk

Charity Registration No. 208223

ISBN 978 1 86203 214 9

Designed and typeset by Soapbox Communications Limited
www.soapboxcommunications.co.uk

Printed and bound in Great Britain by Latimer Trend and Co Ltd

The material selected for the printing of this report is Elemental Chlorine Free and has been sourced from sustainable forests. It has been manufactured by an ISO 14001 certified mill under EMAS.

Contents

	About the Author	4
	Acknowledgments	5
	Executive Summary	6
1	Overview and Historical Context	9
	Increasing competition in Asia during Japan's crisis years	9
	Tokyo still highly ranked as a financial centre	10
2	Japan's Economic Strength	12
3	Big Economy, Big Markets	17
	Second largest stock market	17
	Savings support a large banking sector	19
	The big bond market	20
	The role of foreign assets in international markets and connectedness	23
	Carry trade epitomizes use of short-term trading strategies	24
	Fundamental factors supporting Tokyo's status	25
4	Long-run Risk to the Stock Market?	26
5	Support for Tokyo from Other Markets	29
6	Japan's Banking System after the 2008 Crisis	32
	New opportunities for Japan's banks?	34
7	Market Survey Results and Competitiveness Indicators	36
	Comparative performance of international financial centres	36
	The importance of survey methodologies in determining rankings	37
	Cost-competitiveness indicators	37
	Summary of key points	39
8	Government Policy	40
	Policy recommendations supportive	41
9	Conclusions: Bolder Steps?	43
	International challenges	44

About the Author

Vanessa Rossi is a Senior Research Fellow in International Economics at Chatham House, focusing particularly on international finance, global scenarios and stress testing, including developments in emerging markets. She is a frequent speaker at conferences in London and around the world and on TV and radio. She was previously Director of International Economics for Oxford Economics, helping develop econometric models and detailed analysis of the international economy, the energy sector and capital flows, among other activities. She draws on her extensive experience in international economic analysis and the construction and application of econometric and financial models within the government, university and private sectors, including the European Commission in Brussels, as a research director for Swiss Bank Corporation (now UBS), with consulting groups in the UK and Germany and in academia (Princeton University).

She was co-author of a Chatham House report *The Gulf as a Global Financial Centre: Growing Opportunities and Influence* (June 2008) and contributed to the related Chatham House book edited by John Nugée and Paola Subacchi, *The Gulf Region: A New Hub of Global Financial Power* (November 2008). Other publications include a book on international financial markets and various papers on global economic scenarios and energy demand.

Acknowledgments

Because of the deep relationship between international economic trends, financial market development and government policies, analysis of any part of this triangular relationship requires a holistic understanding of the whole. Chatham House has undertaken a number of projects examining the evolution of financial centres and their relationship with the economic background and policy targets. This latest assessment reviews the position of Tokyo as the centre for Japan's financial services industry. In spite of the grave economic crisis, could this industry succeed in achieving a new breakthrough? Or is it set for long-term decline? In the author's opinion, ongoing incremental adjustments to the current financial services and business environment in Tokyo will be supportive but not transformational – bolder steps should be taken to establish global financial brands leveraged from Japan's large domestic savings base. Such steps may even be facilitated by the present crisis, which has caused asset prices to collapse. The global recession has starkly revealed how large financial centres must have the backing of big, wealthy economies with access to substantial financial resources in order to survive and thrive. One of these centres should be Tokyo.

This study draws on previous analysis of global economic and financial developments and on the very productive and diverse range of meetings held in Japan as well as in London, including detailed discussions with many Japanese experts. Chatham House warmly thanks all who assisted in these meetings and opinion gathering and greatly values their varied inputs, some of which may be recogizable in ideas expressed in this report.

In particular, Chatham House acknowledges the role of the Japan Economic Foundation (JEF) in supporting this project and assisting with the research workshops.

The author greatly appreciates the opportunity to pursue this project, supported by the Research Director, Paola Subacchi, and assisted by Chatham House staff, especially the skillful editing of Margaret May and Nicolas Bouchet.

Thanks also to Taiichiro Tomiyasu, Visiting Fellow, Chatham House for his contribution on the detail of financial trends and government policy initiatives, and to financial market expert Darren Cullen for early discussion of the ideas contained in the report.

And, last but absolutely not least, the author is deeply grateful for the research assistance and many valuable contributions provided by Rodrigo Delgado Aguilera.

The judgments and conclusions, as well as any errors, remain of course the responsibility of the author.

Vanessa Rossi
February 2009

Executive Summary

Tokyo[1] is an important player in the global financial system but it is neither a fully developed global financial centre on a par with New York and London, nor a key hub for the fast-growing 'hinterland' of emerging Asia like Hong Kong and Singapore. As home to Japan's financial institutions and the main conduit for Japan's financial markets and services, serving both the domestic and international markets, Tokyo is the financial heart of Japan. However, compared with London and New York, it is relatively weak in terms of both the presence of foreign financial institutions and the significance and breadth of Japanese financial institutions' operations abroad. The main backing for Tokyo's position as a financial centre is the size of the domestic market, which is in turn supported by the large and wealthy economy. Japan's international business relations have been fostered largely through the expansion of the non-financial corporate sector and global brands in world trade and investment, while the international role of the financial sector, even including the large banks, remains less prominent.

In part, this derives from the fact that Tokyo's role as a financial centre is driven not by growth as an autonomous financial services sector in the same way as London or Singapore, but by Japan's need to fund its corporate sector and generate economic growth in the context of relatively wealthy but extremely risk-averse domestic investors. In spite of a substantial pool of domestic savings, Japan needs a strong mechanism for international financial intermediation in order to resolve its demand-and-supply imbalance across different types of assets. The financial sector must deliver this solution. To ensure that Tokyo can continue to perform this role in the light of expected trends in markets, and current opportunities, Japan should carefully appraise its international strategy. For example, it could look to achieve a higher-profile position in global banking and financial services and to play a greater role in money and bond markets, as well as pursuing the existing policy agenda aimed largely at improving the attractiveness of the equity market and the general business environment in Tokyo.

In spite of the global economic crisis, there are both new opportunities and risks for Tokyo as a centre for international financial services and markets. This report highlights the following factors as key determinants of its future role:

- Tokyo's high ranking as a financial centre, which will continue to be supported by Japan's large financial markets and position as a top-rank economy, boosted by government efforts to implement more market-friendly policies. In spite of concerns about the impact of declining long-run economic growth, Tokyo can remain a top-rank stock market for many years while growth in other markets and services can be pursued both at home and abroad.
- Japan's potential to attract more foreign investment as global interest rates have fallen and investors seek to diversify holdings out of the dollar and euro. This could enhance foreign presence in the Japanese bond market as well as boost the role of the yen and international status of Tokyo.
- The large pool of wealth held both at home and abroad – although this strength needs to be better managed and leveraged, effectively boosting Tokyo's role in financial intermediation and advancing its global influence.
- The scope to mobilize the high levels of cash and bank deposits held by Japanese savers – either by offering incentives for transfers into professional

1 As Tokyo is the dominant financial centre in Japan, with Osaka coming a long way down market survey rankings (as shown later in the report), we do not treat the issue of alternative centres within Japan. The outlook for Tokyo is seen as synonymous with that of Japan in terms of financial-market and services development and the requirements placed on this sector.

fund management products and other investment vehicles (as the government itself has highlighted), or by business development at home and abroad on the part of Japanese banks, insurers and other financial service providers.

- The considerable potential for more strategic long-term management of Japan's substantial capital flows and foreign-asset base, which offers the opportunity to enhance the international influence and reputation of Tokyo's financial sector. The pool of mostly private foreign assets could, and should, play an even more prominent role in boosting Tokyo's status as an international financial centre, for example through the use of this base to build high profile global brands in the international banking, insurance and financial services system.

Risks abound, including the threat of a continued drift away from Tokyo by international financial institutions. This trend could be accelerated by the rising yen, deteriorating cost-competitiveness and a weakening long-run economic growth outlook. This is why Japan needs to take rapid and strategic action, especially in view of the present global crisis.

The key driver is that Tokyo has to be an active international financial centre to achieve the intermediation that Japan requires. In spite of its seemingly ample savings surplus, Japan has to resolve the asset demand-and-supply imbalance associated with the extreme risk aversion of local investors. It needs to invest abroad and, in turn, to attract foreign capital and expertise in financial services to support corporate fundraising and venture capital. This is the key reason for the government's prioritization of policy changes aimed at strengthening the financial services sector and making Tokyo more attractive for foreign investors with a greater appetite for risk than local savers. This imperative to engage in global financial markets could drive Tokyo to become a far more important and highly integrated force in international finance. This pressure is not dissimilar to Japan's need to engage in trade for its companies to expand: once they outgrew their limited home market and resources, they had to become global and, to succeed, they had to be competitive and innovative. Japan's leading manufacturing companies have shown themselves very capable of managing global brands and operations; Tokyo's financial institutions such as banks and insurers can effectively replicate this path, leveraging their substantial base in Japan.

> 'The current crisis has highlighted the growing need for global financial services providers to have the security of a large and solid home base and illustrates the opportunity for Tokyo to shift the balance of power in this sector in its favour'

The current crisis, including the collapse of the Icelandic banking system, has highlighted the growing need for global financial services providers to have the security of a large and solid home base and illustrates the opportunity for Tokyo to shift the balance of power in this sector in its favour. Recent initiatives have been steps in this direction.

It may be tough to argue that Japan's financial institutions should look to expand abroad in the midst of the current exceptional global crisis in financial markets and the world economy, yet the Japanese corporate sector succeeded in doing exactly this during past global recessions. Japan's private-sector foreign assets total about $4–5 trillion. These could be better used to gain strategic advantages in key markets, improve long-run profitability, help resolve Japan's domestic asset demand-and-supply imbalance and foster influence in the global financial sector at a critical time for this industry.

1. Overview and Historical Context

The aim of this study is to critically review the outlook for Tokyo as a financial centre and the role of Japan's financial sector in the light of domestic targets and requirements as well as international trends and competition.

To some extent this assessment is made all the more difficult by the turbulent and damaging effects of the global crisis, which is causing violent swings in financial market data as well as economic conditions. While the final impacts of this severe global recession and subsequent prospects for recovery remain uncertain, it is already clear that Japan's economy has suffered exceptional damage not as a result of the credit crunch *per se* but because of its high level of exposure to the massive downturn in global demand, notably for cars, consumer electronics and investment equipment. The depth of Japan's recession looks set to be far worse than that of the US and the EU bloc.[2]

However, the recession has also radically reshaped the global financial environment in ways that suggest unexpected opportunities for Japanese financial institutions and markets. An immediate example of this is the acquisition by Nomura of parts of Lehman Brothers' operations, which rapidly led to a key advisory role for Nomura in the mid-February 2009 Chinalco-Rio Tinto deal, a major break-through in M&A activity. Another is the sharp reduction in interest rate differentials across the major markets, leaving US and EU yield curves looking remarkably similar to that of Japan. Although these cuts have been driven by the crisis, low rates could persist for longer than the typical cyclical downswing, as Japan discovered in the 1990s. The yen has already benefited from the narrowing in rate differentials, which will also affect the bond market.

This report starts with a brief commentary on the recent background. It then examines the economic backing for Japan's financial markets and the implications of weakening long-run growth trends, before reviewing market positions and developments, the opinions of market participants and other surveys, cost-competitiveness and, finally, the government's policy agenda.[3] The concluding chapter provides summary remarks concerning the likely future trends and opportunities.

Increasing competition in Asia during Japan's crisis years

After the meteoric rise of Japan's economy and financial markets and the yen during the 1980s 'bubble' years – when Tokyo looked set to become Asia's premier financial centre, globally on a par with New York and London – the bursting of the bubble economy at the start of the 1990s delivered a shock not unlike the one that has just hit the US's housing and banking sectors. This 1990s crash severely impaired Japan's financial institutions, non-performing loans (NPLs) soared, the highly inflated stock market plummeted and the banks' capital base was destroyed. Japanese households suffered damage to financial wealth from the stock market collapse and many home-buyers found themselves facing negative equity as house prices fell (although defaults in Japan remained low). This was followed by a protracted restructuring of the banking system and failure to sustain economic recovery – a period that is generally described as a decade of lost opportunity that weakened Japan's internal dynamics and eroded its lead over other Asian financial centres.[4]

2 A Cabinet Office report of 16 February 2009 showed the Japanese economy shrinking at an annualized 12.7% pace for Q4 (over Q3) 2008.

3 Given the impact of the economic and financial crisis in 2008–09, all figures are subject to greater than unusual uncertainty and interpretation, although every care has been taken to check references and calculations. Additionally, slight variations in data may be noticeable when quoted from different sources.

4 This period is described briefly in *The Road to Recovery: A View from Japan* by K. Kang and M. Syed (IMF, 2008) and in depth by Graham Turner in *Solutions to a Liquidity Trap: Japan's Bear Market and What it Means for the West* (GFC Economics, 2003) and *The Credit Crunch* (Pluto Press, 2008), as well as by W. Watanabe, of Keio University in 'How did the flow of funds through the banks change in the 1990s?' (2008). The latest of several publications on the theme of Japan and balance-sheet recessions is *The Holy Grail of Macroeconomics: Lessons from Japan's Great Recession* (John Wiley, 2008) by Richard C. Koo, Nomura Research Institute.

Eventually, the adoption of more radical methods to restart the banking system, lending and economic growth – including bank bail-outs (1998), the zero-interest-rate policy and forced restructuring in the banking sector (2001) – began to achieve modest results, and economic growth gradually improved. Until the onset of the current global recession in 2008, GDP growth was maintained at a steady rate. It averaged around 2% for the five years 2003–07, compared with just 0.2% in the previous five years, which included the deep 1998 recession, and 1.5% in 1993–97, when the economy was rocked by stop-go policies.

Banking-sector capital and balance sheets were strengthened by forced restructuring; non-performing loans were first accounted for and then written off, capital adequacy was improved and there were even the beginnings of a slight recovery in domestic lending from the low point in 2004.[5] Banks' foreign assets also picked up from 2004, rising by about 30% in total by the start of 2008. Reported NPLs peaked at 8.4% in 2002, then fell to 2.4% by March 2008. The capital adequacy ratio rose from just under 10% in 2003 to a peak of more than 13% in March 2007. This improvement in capital was helped by the stock market's rise from a trough in 2003 to a short-term peak in 2007, although it has never regained its 1990 'bubble' peak.

Unfortunately, as the global banking crisis broke in 2007, Japan's equity market started to tumble and it subsequently collapsed to a 26-year low in the turmoil of late 2008. This latest shock has been global rather than centred on Japan but nevertheless the country has been hard hit. This has included fresh damage to banks' capital, leading to new capital-raising exercises. Preliminary data suggest the capital adequacy ratio eased back to about 12.3% in March 2008, and a further steep fall is expected in 2009. NPLs also picked up in September 2008.

During the recovery years up to 2008, profitability also improved although this had to struggle against the headwinds caused by the low 'nominal' environment – that is, near-zero inflation and interest rates which make it difficult for banks to earn fees and raise margins. The international banks generally find it easier to achieve better margins and fees in economies with a higher 'nominal' environment, such as the US or UK, which has encouraged some global banks to expand into these markets. Japanese banks also operate abroad but their expansion seems to have been very slow, largely serving the international requirements of Japanese companies.

However, Japan's banks were only just emerging from restructuring in 2005–07 as the new wave of problems for the global banking system began to develop. There was insufficient time to regain the momentum lost during the crisis years, although, more positively, this also meant that the Japanese banks largely avoided the sub prime and derivatives disasters that have struck US and European banks.[6]

Tokyo still highly ranked as a financial centre

Tokyo remains highly ranked as a financial centre, whether this is judged objectively by size of markets, market activity and wealth or by other indicators of performance such as market opinion polls and commissioned reports. In the City of London's *Global Financial Centres Index 4 (GFCI4)* published in September 2008, Tokyo was placed seventh overall, jumping up from ninth in the previous survey of spring 2008. In the World Economic Forum's *Financial Development Report* of 2008, Japan as a whole ranked even higher (fourth). This is due in large part to the WEF's added emphasis on market development rather than competitiveness (which tends to be strongly influenced by market participants who are typically critical of Japan's regulatory and tax systems, among other common complaints).

Nevertheless, Tokyo's position is being challenged largely because Japan appears to be at risk of being eclipsed as an economic power by the rise of the rest of Asia, specifically China but also, on a more distant horizon, India. There has been increasingly stiff competition among rival financial centres, including new challenges posed by developing centres such as Shanghai, Mumbai and the Gulf states as well as old rivals Hong Kong and Singapore – all of which offer easy access to emerging Asia as well as cheaper operating and living costs than Tokyo.[7]

The rise of Hong Kong and Singapore was made easier by the additional benefits they could offer in terms of existing experience in financial markets with strong links to London

5 Tables detailing these data are provided in the government policy review in Chapter 8.

6 See Chapter 6 for further discussion of this issue.

7 Further evidence on this point is also provided in Chapter 7.

and New York, recognized institutions and very competitive taxes and operating regimes; the authorities were always under pressure owing to the rivalry between the two centres over which would be the dominant hub in emerging Asia.

Table 1: World financial centre rankings

	GFCI4		WEF
1	London	1	United States
2	New York	2	United Kingdom
3	Singapore	3	Germany
4	Hong Kong	4	Japan
5	Zurich	5	Canada
6	Geneva	6	France
7	Tokyo	7	Switzerland
8	Chicago	8	Hong Kong
9	Frankfurt	9	Netherlands
10	Sydney	10	Singapore

Sources: City of London, WEF

Intermediation within Asian domestic markets (between savers/borrowers, households/corporates) typically takes place within the large local banking sectors. Low-cost deposit bases support large banks and bank lending, which overshadows the region's small, undeveloped debt markets. However, stock markets are relatively well developed as there is greater support for an equity culture. In this respect, emerging Asia is very similar to Japan. Foreign participation in emerging Asia has tended to focus heavily on foreign direct investment (unlike Japan) but there are also sizeable portfolio flows into regional stock markets. This reflects the relative importance of trade and related investment in Asia but also the build-up of an international investor base alongside the region's rapid economic expansion. In terms of competition in financial services, widespread Asian expertise in both banking and equities means that Japan has little advantage in these markets and related services compared with its Asian neighbours. However, it is unique in having a large debt market and the yen is a key international reserve currency even though its share has more than halved since the end of the bubble economy.

Tokyo failed to secure a dominant position in Asian finance during the important development stages for regional growth and finance in the 1990s, which coincided with Japan's prolonged economic and financial crisis – indeed, the withdrawal of Japanese banks from Asian markets as balance sheets were forced to contract was seen at the time as one of the possible triggers for the onset of the Asian crisis in 1997–98. Tokyo has subsequently struggled to regain momentum in the international context and relies heavily on the support provided by its large home markets.

Amidst concern over the potential erosion of Japan's long-term position in global finance and Japanese companies' ability to raise capital, which would both reflect and exacerbate weak underlying economic trends, the government has been actively promoting a plan aimed at invigorating growth prospects by stimulating the environment for both the corporate and the financial sectors.[8] The main focus of concern has been the regulatory framework, which tends to be widely quoted by market surveys and research reports as a negative factor for Japan's financial market development and status as a financial centre.[9] There is likely to be further supportive action from the authorities following a raft of regulatory changes in 2008[10] although the need to tackle the current economic crisis along with uncertainty over political leadership (with elections widely expected in 2009) will delay and dilute policy changes, especially regarding the potential to implement any changes in the area of taxation. In addition, the outbreak of the global crisis has changed some of the parameters under which Tokyo operates: this may offer some unexpected advantages compared with other financial centres in spite of causing widespread distress in Japan's economy.

In the light of these changes in background conditions, can Tokyo engineer a renaissance as a leading international financial centre or will it gradually fall back in the rankings, becoming increasingly isolated as it caters mainly for 'home-biased' and increasingly conservative domestic investors? Is the government right to be concerned about Japan's position in financial markets and its impact on economic growth? The next chapters examine the key swing factors before considering actions that might promote a more positive outcome.

8 Japanese Financial Services Agency (JFSA), 'Strengthening the Competitiveness of Japan's Financial and Capital Markets', December 2007.
9 Taxation is another issue raised but changes in this respect would be more difficult to implement, especially in the near term.

2. Japan's Economic Strength

Table 2: Rankings by GDP ($ trillion)

Rank	Region	GDP estimates $tn 2007	2017
1	EU (inc UK)	17	24
2	US	14	21
3	Japan	4.4	6
4	China	3.4	12
5-9	Canada, Brazil, Russia, India, Korea	1-1.5	India 3
=10	GCC total, Mexico, Australia	0.8-1	Average about 2
	World total	54-55	95-100

GCC = Gulf Cooperation Council states

Sources: IMF, World Bank, national statistics offices and own estimates

- Japan will remain in the top 4 by size of GDP even after China overtakes it in 2010–11
- The next tier are a long way behind, unlikely to overtake Japan before 2030
- Data at market exchange rates, not PPP

Even after almost twenty years of mediocre growth, Japan's economy still ranks as the third largest in the world by size of GDP after the US and EU (number two on a country basis, ahead of China and Germany). China will soon overtake Japan in terms of national GDP,[11] but any other challengers are a long way behind, suggesting that Japan probably has twenty years, possibly more, before there will be a contender for fourth place. India is expected to catch up before 2030 and other competition may depend on a sustained resurgence in energy and commodity prices to boost the oil economies and Brazil.

Figure 1: Share of world GDP by country (MER constant 1993 prices)

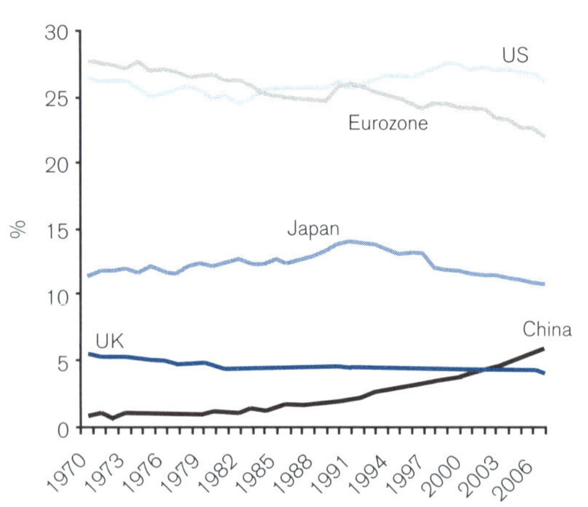

Source: UN

Nevertheless, in spite of Japan's economy remaining in the top rank, its share of global GDP is already declining and will decrease further over the long run. The current share is estimated at 8–9% but this is forecast to fall to about 7% by 2020.[12] The trend is important not just as an indicator of economic power in the world order but also as a signal for the financial sector's growth and financial market rankings. For example, the equity market share in global market capitalization tends to be strongly correlated with the GDP share (as discussed later, see Figure 14). Thus the current position, in which Japan represents about 8% of the value of global equities, looks set to decline in tandem with its share in global GDP over the long run. The implications for the stock market are discussed later in Chapter 4.

Japan also plays a key role in world trade, coming just behind the EU, the US and China in terms of export and import sales. This active role in trade is important in promoting related international financial services and investment, capital flows and trading in the yen. It indicates the degree of 'openness' of the country in both a narrow and broad sense, boosting its potential to act as an

11 GDP at market exchange rates (MER) – in purchasing power parity adjusted terms, China has already surpassed Japan.

12 Also measured at market exchange rates (MER), not PPP – although the estimate varies according to the form of the data used (constant or current prices).

Figure 2: Trade rankings by exports and imports (2007)

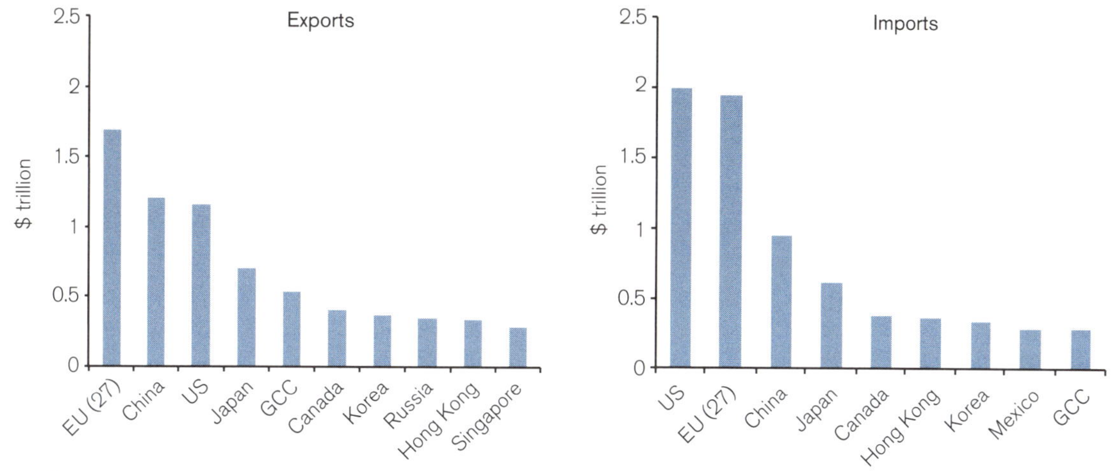

Source: WTO

international financial centre. The most important current examples of this leveraging of a position as a trade hub to promote financial hub activities are Hong Kong and Singapore, but it was also one important historical reason for the rise of London and New York and, before that, the growth of banking and finance in the Italian states during the expansion of trade in the pre-industrial era.

Japan's ability to maintain a dominant position in world trade may therefore be as important, arguably even more important, for its role in international financial markets than its ranking in terms of GDP.

Of course, growth in global trade is also a strategy for the corporate sector to grow faster than the limits imposed by a slow-growing domestic economy – boosting corporate power and therefore the potential rating of Japan's equity market.

In spite of the competitive threat from the rest of Asia and the rapid transfer of some industries to lower-cost bases, chiefly in China, Japan has continued to see robust growth in its manufacturing industry and exports (excluding the impact of the current recession). However, the financial sector and other services have fared less well, having failed to sustain expansion abroad during the 1990s. Indeed, service exports have been generally weak, pointing to broader problems of competitiveness in services, not just in the financial sector. If this trend is not addressed and improved, it could threaten to erode the standing of Tokyo over the long run.

The yen's appeal as the fourth most important international reserve currency, and a potential 'safe haven' along with the dollar, euro, pound and Swiss franc, is also well supported by Japan's high ranking in terms of GDP and trade, backed up by a strong international balance-of-payments position and the Bank of Japan's substantial foreign exchange reserves of close to $1 trillion. The latter credentials, in particular, may even serve to boost the yen's international role in the aftermath of the 2008–09 crisis.

Importantly for financial services development, and thanks to historically high levels of savings, Japan is a major contributor to world wealth, representing around 15% of estimated global financial wealth (on 2007 data), almost double its share of 8–9% in global GDP. This is reflected in the development of Japan's large domestic markets: bank deposits are worth approximately $9 trillion, equivalent to about double annual GDP, while the stock market capitalization is roughly aligned with annual GDP (both around $4.5 trillion), making it the second largest market in the world after the US.

In addition, Japan is the only significant Asian country to have not only a well-developed banking system and equity market but also, unusually, a very large domestic bond market. In total, this market is also worth around double annual GDP, or $9–10 trillion. It is composed of corporate debt (including Samurai bonds issued by emerging market economies), local government debt and central government debt, which accounts for about $7–8 trillion of the market. Government debt built up rapidly during the post-bubble years of large public-sector deficits and banking-sector restructuring. In the mid-1990s the budget deficit ballooned and has remained in the 5–10% of GDP range for most years since; indeed the impact of recession will lead to a renewed rise.

Domestically generated financial market wealth is therefore equivalent to about five times GDP. Around two-thirds of this represents household wealth, the result of a long build-up of savings, as well as high returns on investments during the bubble years. Although the household savings rate (as a percentage of household income) has drifted down from around 20% in the early 1980s to 10–15% in the 1990s (even dipping below 10% in recent years), savings have remained much higher than the low US rate and about on a par with the rate in Germany or France.

In addition to domestic assets, foreign investments, including foreign exchange (FX) reserves of nearly $1 trillion, are also worth $5–6 trillion. Taking into account around $2 trillion in foreign investments in Japan, net foreign wealth is therefore $3–4 trillion. In total, Japanese financial wealth is estimated to be almost six times GDP. While estimates vary slightly based on valuation methods, dates and the exchange rate for the yen, overall net wealth was probably around $27–29 trillion based on 2007–08 data.

Table 3: Estimated distribution of world wealth ($ trillion)

Country/Region	1997	2007	2017
Top 3	75	160	315
US	33	65	120
EU (inc UK)	25	65	150
Japan	17	30	45
Rest	17	40	95
China	3-5	10-11	30
GCC	1-2	4-5	15
Global Total	92	200	410

Sources: IMF historical data and own estimates (rounded)

The build-up of Japan's *foreign wealth* has been due to positive *net national savings*, as represented by the persistent surplus on the current account of the balance of payments, which has varied within the $50–200 billion per annum range since the mid-1980s. Japan has persistently saved more than it consumes and has therefore accumulated a large stock of foreign assets managed by the private

Figure 3: Japanese public debt and deficit levels

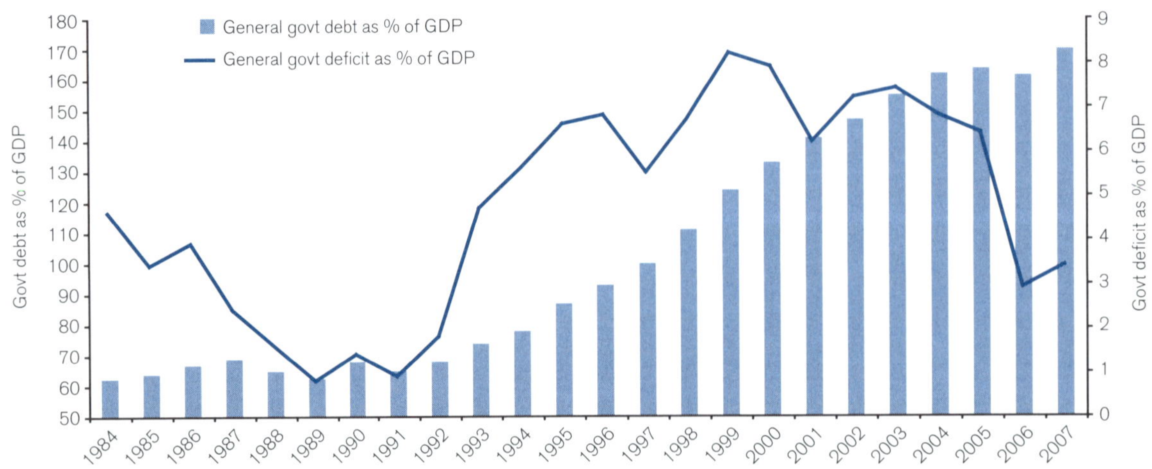

Sources: Japanese Ministry of Finance, OECD

Figure 4: Japanese and key emerging markets current accounts and global imbalances by region

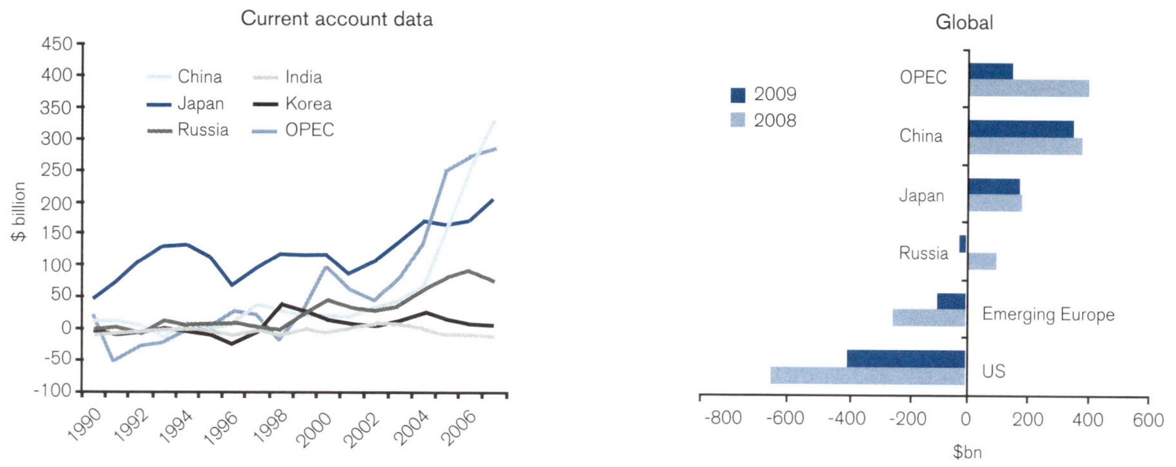

Sources: IFS, official national data, author's estimates.

sector and in FX reserves at the central bank. While the present crisis may reduce this national surplus, owing to losses in net export revenues, Japan is likely to retain a surplus on the current account during the downturn, and a structural surplus is expected to persist in the long run as well (although the level may start to decline). In addition, the overall balance of payments will be boosted by the drying up of Japan's typically large capital outflows as investors react to the global crisis by keeping more funds at home.

Japan's shares in world financial wealth are considerably larger than its share in world GDP – indeed, estimating total global 'international' wealth (wealth held outside 'home' markets) at around $25–30 trillion, then Japan's share of this wealth is as much as 20%, almost the same as that of the US or EU. Other countries' FX reserves also account for about 20%, with sovereign wealth funds (SWFs) and other private wealth accounting for the remaining 20%. Excluding official holdings of foreign assets, *Japan has the largest pool of privately held foreign assets in the world.*

Figure 5: Japanese shares of world wealth

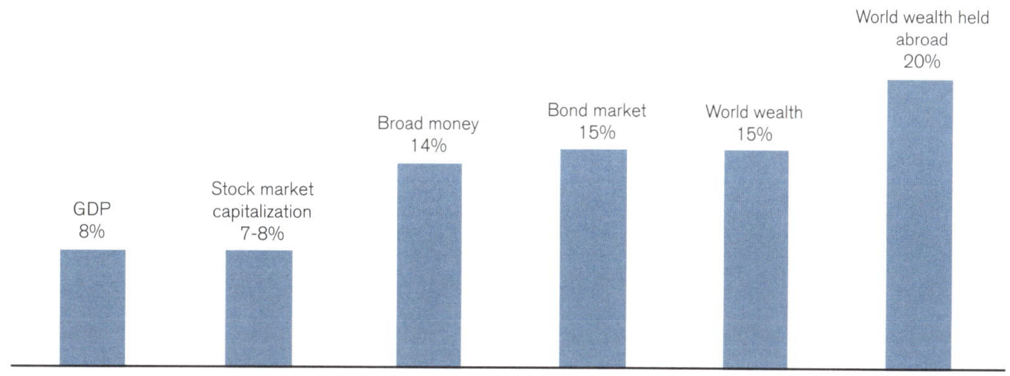

Sources: Data estimated from various market statistics and world estimates, shares confirmed by other sources

Japan scores less well in terms of attracting wealth into the country: this totals around $2 trillion, less than 8% of the estimated pool of 'international' wealth. More than half of this foreign investment – some $1–1.5 trillion – is held in the form of equity investments. The overall figure is depressed by weak foreign interest in the bond market – a more balanced weighting in this market would significantly boost overall foreign investment in Japan to as much as $3–5 trillion.

3. Big Economy, Big Markets

The size and ranking of Japan's financial markets derive mainly from Japan's economic status as a large, developed and wealthy economy, as illustrated in Figure 6.

Second largest stock market

Most of the foreign interest in Japan's financial markets has been due to investments in the large stock market, the world's second largest by capitalization, which is roughly in line with Japan's total annual GDP (and about the same share of the world total, around 8–9%, as world stock market capitalization is roughly 100% of world GDP). This large equity market is supported by Japan's commensurately large corporate sector. Japan's global companies also derive an important part of their revenues and profits from abroad, which helps support high stock market values and growth in spite of relatively low national GDP growth. However, this foreign exposure implies that profits and equity values are highly vulnerable to swings in the international economy, trade and currencies – such as the downturn that started in 2008. It is not surprising, therefore, that Japan's stock market plunged along with other markets worldwide in response to the global recession even before the full scale of the damage to the domestic economy was known. Global sales, operations and earnings mean that companies' share prices will be affected by the economic performance of trade partners.

Apart from stock market capitalization and performance, other key statistics also indicate the importance of

Figure 6: Japan's big markets – key statistics

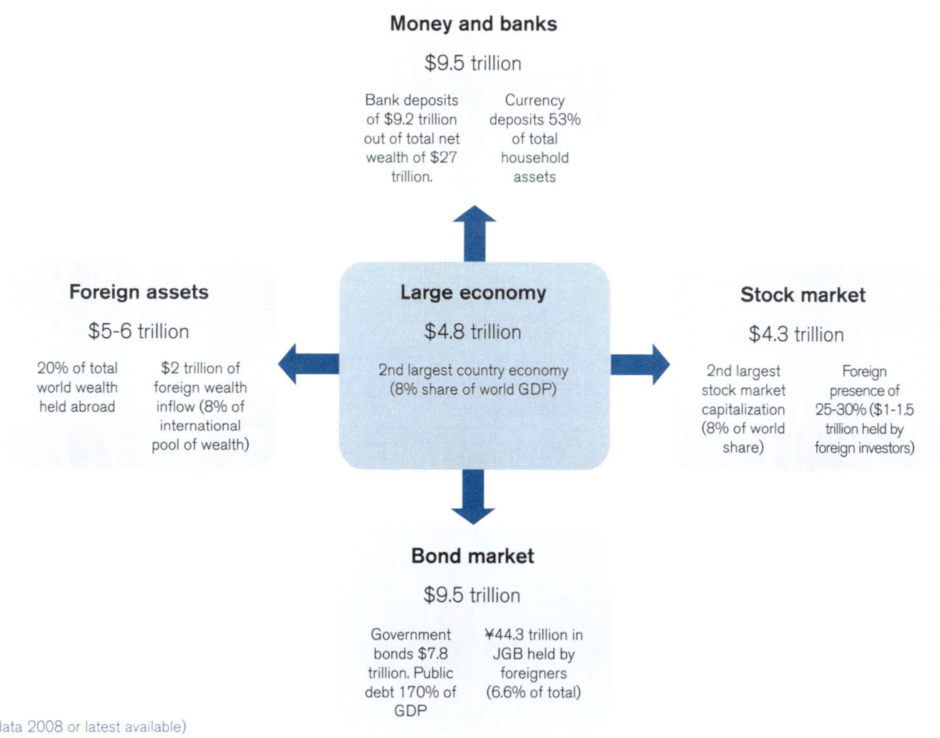

Source: Author (data 2008 or latest available)

the Japanese stock market: these include very high levels of turnover and the large number of companies listed, although foreign listings are relatively low.

Table 4: Comparison of world stock markets

	Market capitalization ($ trillions)	Market capitalization (% WFE)	Share trading (% WFE)	Listed companies
Japan	4.3	7.1	6.4	2,414
Hong Kong	2.7	4.4	2.1	1,241
Singapore	0.5	0.9	0.4	762
Australia	1.3	2.1	1.4	1,998
US*	19.7	32.3	44.7	5,366
UK	3.9	6.3	10.2	3.307
Euronext	4.2	6.9	5.6	1,155
World (WFE Total)	60.9			

*NYSE/Nasdaq

Source: World Federation of Exchanges *Annual Report 2007*

As well as having substantial stock market activity and a large number of listed companies, Japan ranks highly in terms of private equity deals. It is a long way behind the US but still has a significant presence compared with any other countries, including Europe.

Table 5: Global private equity investment

	$bn, value of investment		% share	
	2006	*2007*	*2006*	*2007*
US	347	485	70	71
UK	51	47	10	7
France	13	17	3	2
Sweden	4	10	1	2
Spain	5	6	1	1
Germany	3	5	1	1
Netherlands	4	4	1	1
Japan	**66**	**111**	**13**	**16**
Others	494	686	100	100

Source: International Financial Services, London (IFSL)

Another, rather mixed, indicator of the competitiveness of Japan's financial sector and its role in global equity markets is the scale of mergers and acquisitions (M&A) activity and number of deals undertaken by Japanese institutions.

Although Japan's share of worldwide M&A is not particularly large, it nevertheless rates highly relative to that of most other countries – it is sixth in the world behind the US and UK (which together account for over half the global share), Canada, France and Germany. In terms of the actual number of M&A deals, its share is even larger and trails only the US and the UK. Despite the high relative position of Japan in M&A market share, the transaction value of these activities relative to GDP is quite low. This suggests that Japan's relatively high world shares have more to do with the large size of its market than the importance of M&A deals among its financial activities as a whole. At the same time, the figures for Hong Kong and Singapore benefit from their advantageous position in Chinese and Asian markets.

Overall, the figures serve to reinforce the perception among investors that Japan is weak in M&A activity, given its low share in this segment compared with the size of its economy. Clearly M&A is a business dominated by the major US and European banks and highly concentrated in the US and UK. Emphasizing this point is a restrictive legal environment, high tax rates, resistance towards hostile takeovers and the fact that no major Japanese bank was among the top ten advisers in global M&A deals in 2008.[13] This, however, may change as the current financial crisis has allowed Japanese institutions new opportunities for global expansion in the wake of declining market valuations overseas. In recent months, Nomura, Mizuho, SMFG and Mitsubishi UFJ have all claimed stakes in overseas institutions including Merrill Lynch, Barclays and Morgan Stanley. More recently, Nomura (through its acquisition of Lehman Brothers' European and Asian M&A assets) secured a role as lead adviser to Chinalco's $19.5 billion investment in Rio Tinto, the largest ever foreign investment by a Chinese company and one which has been described as among the 'most complex and politically charged deals ever seen'.[14]

13 Dealogic data for Q3 2008.

14 *Financial Times*, 12 September 2008, 'It's time to leave home again', and 13 February 2009, 'Foreign Lehman team leads on Chinalco'.

Figure 7: M&A transaction value to GDP

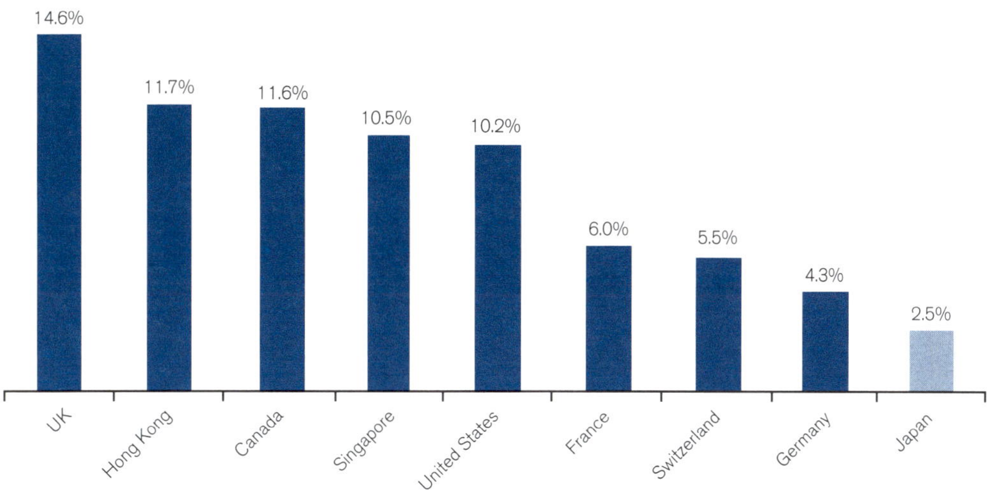

Source: WEF *Financial Development Report 2008*

Table 6: M&A activity as share of world total

	By $ value (share)	%		By number (share)	%
1	USA	44.4	1	USA	33.2
2	UK	11.3	2	UK	9.5
3	Canada	4.8	3	Japan	6.3
4	France	4.4	4	Australia	5.2
5	Germany	4.1	5	Canada	5.2
6	Japan	3.6	6	Germany	4.7

Source: WEF *Financial Development Report 2008*

Savings support a large banking sector

Apart from maintaining a large, highly rated stock market, the level of domestic savings also supports a large banking sector by supplying a substantial, low-cost deposit base. Bank deposits represent a very high share of household wealth (over 50%) compared with other countries, indicating the degree of risk aversion among Japanese savers, in part a legacy of the post-bubble years. The high level of liquidity (excess savings) places a considerable onus on the banks to raise lending and act as the intermediaries in corporate finance. However, their caution linked to previous years of crisis has perhaps tended to make the banking sector a reluctant lender, damping down the velocity (circulation rate) of money in the Japanese economy and potentially leaving the corporate sector undersupplied with funds in spite of the high domestic savings base. Awareness of the longer-term risks posed by this structure of high levels of liquidity and possibly excessive caution over lending have led the government to examine this issue, resulting in a recommendation to find ways to encourage more households to hold wealth in managed funds rather than in bank accounts.

Table 7: Public debt as percentage of GDP (2008)

Rank	Country	Public debt % of GDP
1	Zimbabwe	241.2
2	Lebanon	190.5
3	Japan	170.4*
4	Jamaica	124.1
5	Italy	103.7
23	US	60.8
43	UK	47.2

* Levels for government debt quoted vary considerably depending on inclusion or exclusion of local government debt and whether the debt is quoted as gross or net. The lowest estimates for net debt tend to be around 100% of GDP and a commonly quoted figure for the current gross debt is 160–170%.

Source: *CIA World Factbook*

Figure 8: Relative size of financial markets and wealth ($tn)

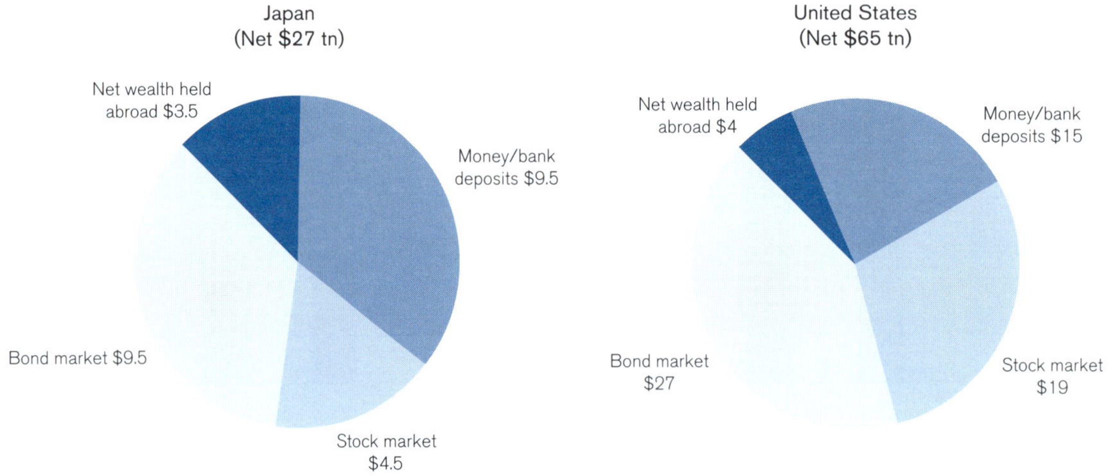

Sources: BIS, IMF, WFE. Estimates rounded.

Figure 9: Comparison of households' asset holdings

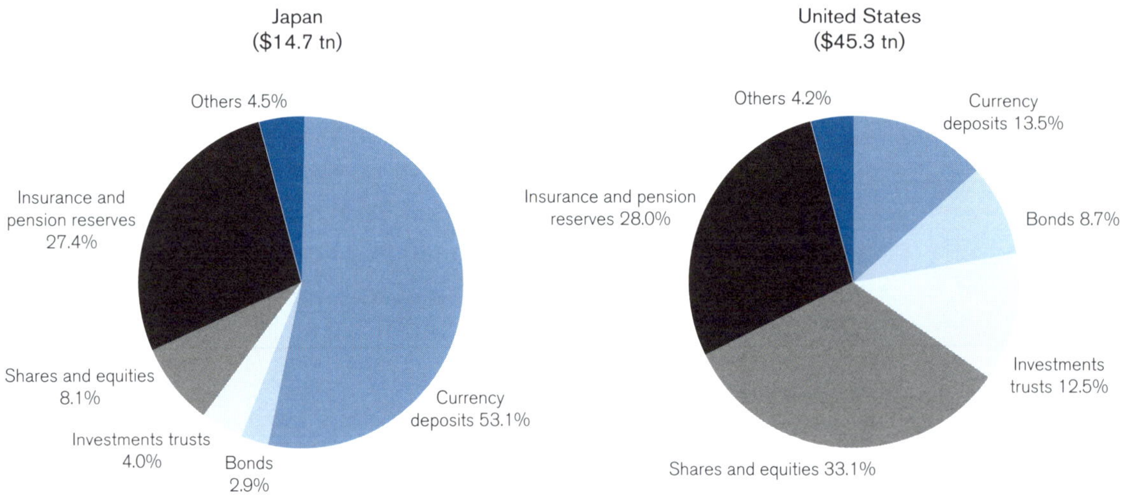

Source: JFSA, September 2008

Change may be hard to achieve without jeopardizing financial security, however, and households will be even more reluctant to shift out of secure deposits in view of the current global economic and financial crisis. Moreover, Japan's persistently low inflation rate means there is less pressure on households to move into assets such as equities to gain protection from inflation. It is also more difficult for banks to make profits under low inflation and interest rate regimes – they do better in mildly inflationary environments – but this is one reason why the banks may press ahead with international expansion. This could improve profitability as well as balancing their otherwise heavy exposure to the Japanese corporate loans market.

The big bond market

In addition to swelling bank accounts, the high level of domestic savings has provided ample support for a large and still growing government bond market. High levels of government deficit spending have been maintained well beyond the 'lost decade', racking up a large public-sector debt that has reached 160–170% of GDP. In 2008, Japan had the largest ratio of public-sector debt to GDP in the developed world. Indeed its government was not far off being the world's number one debtor.

While many market participants and economists see this elevated level of public-sector debt as a burden and a serious risk factor for Japan (for example, the government debt position is mentioned in the City of London surveys and in the WEF report), this view may be misleading and should be challenged. Although concern over large deficits and rising debt was rampant in the mid-1990s – and led to a notably disastrous attempt to claw back spending and raise taxes in 1997 – Japan has subsequently learned to live with its large debt market without suffering a government debt crisis, or, indeed, seeing escalating 'costs' in the form of rising interest rates. Both interest rates and bond yields have remained low – and it was obviously not the scale of Japan's government debt that brought about the present crisis and devastating recession in Japan.

Apart from reduced concern over the scale of public-sector debt, another factor that is turning international comparisons in Japan's favour, in relative terms, is the impact of the economic crisis on many other countries' fiscal deficits and debt. Public-sector debt is expected to balloon around the world as the previously unthinkable becomes the new orthodoxy for fiscal policy responses to the crisis. Faced with the necessities to pay for large bank bail-outs, to support collapsing companies and to limit the rise in unemployment by job creation, public-sector spending will rise sharply at the same time as tax revenues are plummeting. Even countries that see no scope for increasing spending, owing to already high deficits and debt, will inevitably see their public-sector deficits hit by severe tax revenue losses. While countries with strong public-sector finances and the backing of high national savings may be able to weather these impacts on their financial systems, the weak will lapse into crisis and face rising interest rates as risk premiums soar – indeed, this divergence in risk profiles is already showing up across global markets, including across the Eurozone countries. Compared with these rising risks across international economies and markets, Japan is notably well placed to be able to fund its public-sector debt at relatively low interest rates in spite of the crisis – setting it apart as a relatively secure market in the midst of the financial storm.

'Compared with these rising risks across international economies and markets, Japan is notably well placed to be able to fund its public-sector debt at relatively low interest rates in spite of the crisis – setting it apart as a relatively secure market in the midst of the financial storm'

In addition, the large bond market makes Japan unique in Asia – the Japanese government bond market alone (approximately $8 trillion and including a sizeable share of local government bonds), is larger than the market for marketable US Treasury securities. On the other hand, other non-government bonds (financial and corporate) are relatively small, totalling approximately $1 trillion, which means the high-risk component of the total bond market is very low – in the US, the corporate debt market is roughly double the government bond market.

This large bond market could be seen as a considerable advantage, especially given the firm support provided by a substantial pool of domestic savings and strong 'home- biased' demand for conservative 'secure' investments in yen. Japan need not rely on foreign borrowing to fund its debt – indeed it is a supplier of capital to the rest of the world, and foreign participation in the bond market is low. This relative security, along with other factors, has meant that Japan's bond market has been able to maintain low yields in spite of the high level of debt/GDP.

Japan is well placed to participate in the development of bond markets in Asia if this asset class becomes more attractive following the crash in global equity markets. The global recession and growing counter-cyclical fiscal spending suggest most countries will see government borrowing rise – necessitating the issuance of new debt.

Figure 10: Size and structure of world bond markets

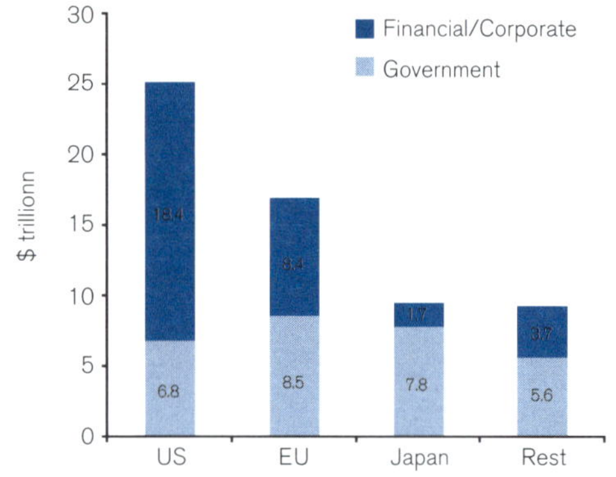

Source: BIS

Reflecting the status of the Japanese economy and the backing provided by its financial markets and wealth, the yen is regarded as an important international currency. The yen plays an important role in global FX trading: it is the third most traded currency behind the US dollar and the euro even though its share of total turnover has dropped to a level only marginally higher than that of the next contender, the UK pound. Although reflective of Japan's post-bubble downturn and the decline in the share of dollar/yen trades, this fall in share of turnover is also associated with the overall diversification of FX trading in recent years, with significant increases in emerging market currencies such as the Hong Kong dollar (itself largely benefiting from China's economic expansion). Apart from FX trading, the yen is also among the key international currencies held in central bank FX portfolios, although here too its share has fallen, more than halving since the mid-1990s. It has recently trailed the pound sterling in addition to the US dollar and euro (both of which, combined, account for as much as 90% of all holdings). However, the existence of a large bond market in Japan supports the use of the yen rather than other Asian units as an international reserve currency.

One obstacle to the yen playing a larger role in both private investment strategies and central bank reserve holdings has been the very low level of Japanese interest rates, which has encouraged large private capital outflows, thus weakening the yen. Interestingly, this position is now changing as world interest rates have tumbled towards Japanese levels, capital has flowed back to Japan and the yen has soared. We will return to this point in discussing the outlook for Japan's bond market.

Figure 11: Share of world FX trading and reserves

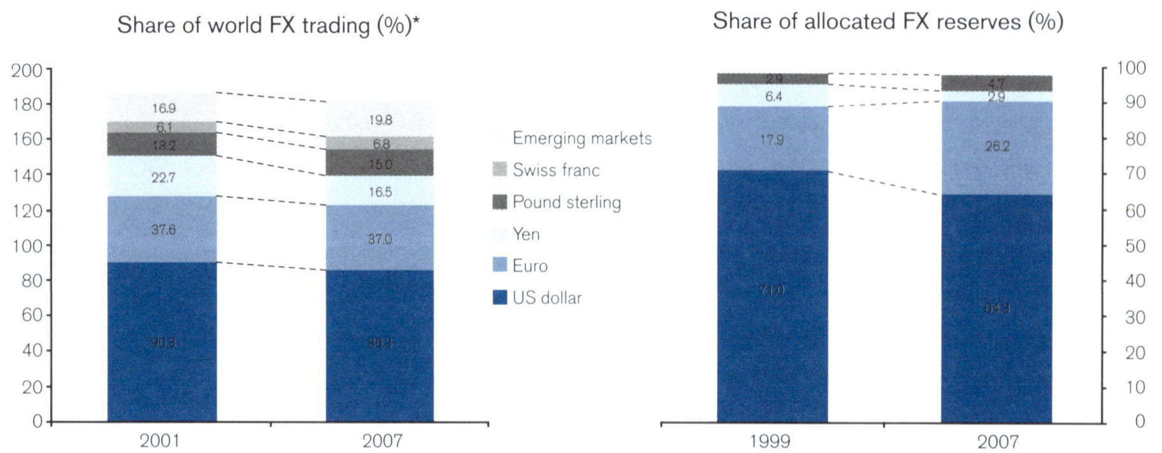

* Because two currencies are involved in each transaction, the sum of the percentage shares of individual currencies totals 200% instead of 100%.

Sources: BIS, IMF

The role of foreign assets international markets and connectedness

While the most important underlying determinant of Tokyo's current position as an international financial centre derives from the sheer size of the national economy, savings and domestic financial markets, its role in international markets and its status with international investors are also key issues in assessing the overall ranking and outlook as a financial centre. Size of domestic markets is only one of the factors supporting a successful international financial centre and service industries.

Another important feature is 'interconnectedness' with other markets and global finance. In this respect, Tokyo benefits from the presence of foreign banks and financial services companies as well as the influx of foreign investment into its markets.

Figure 12: Foreign banks and listed companies

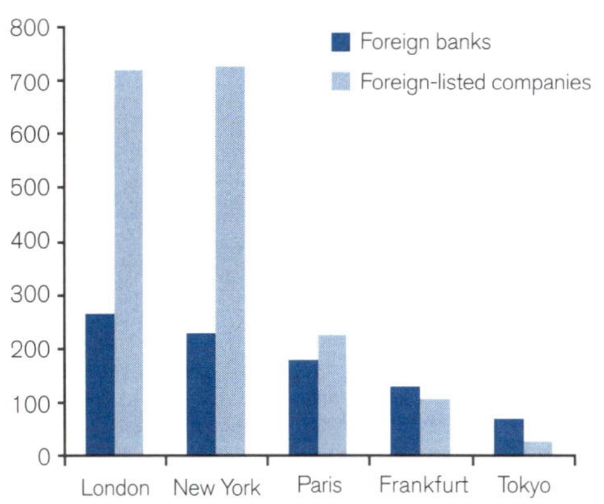

Sources: WFE, ISFL

The record in terms of foreign participation in Japan is, however, mixed. The most important foreign presence is the 25–30% share of the equity market, and yen trading. Other indicators are less favourable. For example, there is very little participation in the bond market (only 6–7% held by foreign investors to 2008), which is supported by local investors and institutions; and the number of foreign banks and financial institutions physically present in Tokyo is low (and has actually been declining).

Additionally, there are only 25 foreign-listed companies on the Tokyo stock exchange (just 1% of the total of 2,414); this compares unfavourably with other financial centres even in the Asia-Pacific region.[15]

Concern that foreign participation will continue to wane has been one of the motivating factors behind government attempts to examine and address complaints about the Japanese markets and the environment for financial services businesses (policies discussed in Chapter 8).

The role of foreign assets in international markets and connectedness

Another important aspect of Japan's connectedness with international financial markets and other centres is the role played by Japan's large holdings of foreign financial assets and the impact that management of these assets has on other markets. Excluding investments such as property holdings, Japanese investors and the Bank of Japan (FX reserves) combined have accumulated around $5–6 trillion in financial assets abroad, compared with foreign holdings in Japan (largely the stock market) worth only $2 trillion.

Japan's stock of foreign financial assets is therefore almost on par with equivalent figures for the US (and Eurozone) and larger than either the total for emerging market FX reserves (about $4.5 trillion) or the combined assets of SWFs (about $3–4 trillion, as estimated before the recent crash in asset prices).

However, there are important differences between the varying objectives and management styles of the private investors behind Japan's stock of foreign assets – which fragments the power of this block of wealth in world markets – and the more concentrated holdings and powerful influence of central banks and SWFs. While there has been considerable interest in the activities and impact of SWFs and central bank FX reserves, far less interest has been shown in Japan's much larger private foreign asset base and its impact on world markets.

Nevertheless, capital outflows from Japan may play a disproportionately large role in certain types of transactions in international markets – for example, in trading of

15 Foreign-listed companies for other major Asia-Pacific financial centres include Sydney (85), Singapore (290) and Hong Kong (9).

high-yield emerging-market currencies. Japan's foreign investments may have marked implications for some parts of the world. More importantly, especially given the large pool of private wealth involved, there may be better ways of professionally managing these external funds from the point of view of the individual wealth holders, for example, to reduce risk and volatility in returns. This might also reduce the turbulence caused in other countries' markets by the entry and exit of Japanese short-term financial investments – and reduce yen volatility as well.

Carry trade epitomizes use of short-term trading strategies

In recent years, Japan's pool of foreign investments has been augmented by so-called 'carry trade', capital outflows generated by investors borrowing in 'cheap' yen (at very low short-term interest rates) to invest outside Japan (borrowing has largely been transacted through the banking system and may, in part, represent transactions on the part of non-Japanese institutions and individual investors). This investment activity has typically been seen as aiming for short-term trading profits in high-yield currencies and other speculative positions.

> 'Further large inflows of capital back to Japan could risk pushing the yen higher, above tolerance thresholds given the crisis already hitting Japan's economy and manufacturing base'

The cumulated stock of carry trade investments is estimated to have reached around $300–400 billion[16] at its peak, based on annual outflows of some $50-100 billion over 2005–07. This total is quite small compared with Japan's overall foreign asset base, and carry trade may well represent only a temporary arbitrage phenomenon in capital markets. However, the approach to foreign investment epitomizes the way in which short-term trading strategies operate and influence markets. It is possible that a large part of Japan's private foreign asset base of $4–5 trillion is invested in a similar way, with consequently volatile returns for investors and potentially destabilizing impacts on currencies, including the yen. This contrasts with long-term investments designed to return a steady income flow with less churning of underlying assets and less risk to the value of the capital invested – for example, the long-term holdings of the central bank in US government bonds. However, the risks associated with carry trade and similar short-term investments are perhaps best illustrated not by the impact of their growth but by the consequences of their reversal.

Under the influence of growing uncertainty and turmoil in global markets, growth in carry trade borrowing came to a halt during 2008, and may possibly have gone into reverse. This is seen as contributing to the rise in the yen, together with repatriation of other short-term funds held abroad and the drying up of capital outflows. However, it seems unlikely (on present information and data) that carry trade and other short-term investments have completely reversed yet. Further large inflows of capital back to Japan could risk pushing the yen higher, above tolerance thresholds given the crisis already hitting Japan's economy and manufacturing base. Pressure to avoid this happening implies recourse to emergency intervention if needed, pushing up central bank FX reserves. This would effectively transfer part of Japan's foreign asset base from the private sector and into central bank holdings of US and EU government bonds.

Carry trade is a specific example of how low Japanese interest rates have tended to encourage large speculative capital flows. The experience of yen volatility in crises (1998 was another example) illustrates the hazards associated with the sudden unwinding of capital flows.

Such risks raise questions over the appropriateness of Japan's external fund management, suggesting the need to

16 Own estimates and quotes from JPMorgan research.

encourage longer-term strategic holdings that reduce the threat of unacceptable volatility for the yen, Japanese investors and the recipient countries of Japanese capital flows. Consolidation of the large pool of private foreign assets into larger fund management operations could serve to enhance the reputation and influence of Tokyo's financial services sector in international markets.

An alternative strategy could be pursued through the international expansion of Japanese banks – this would also serve to stabilize foreign asset holdings and capital flows, as well as enabling the banks to improve lending margins compared with the domestic market.

Fundamental factors supporting Tokyo's status

To summarize, three fundamental factors supporting Tokyo's current status as a financial centre have been identified in the arguments presented above:

- *The large economy, including strength in world trade and significant levels of financial wealth, supports large domestic financial markets:* this provides solid backing for the corporate sector and the equity market as well as the banking sector and bond market. Japan's stock market capitalization is the world's second largest, representing around 7–9% of the global equity market, roughly the same as Japan's share in global GDP.[17] There is also a significant foreign presence in this market, with 25–30% (around $1–1.5 trillion) held by foreign investors.
- *The important role played by the yen in global FX trading* – it is ranked third in terms of turnover share and is the fourth most important international currency in central banks' FX portfolios after the US dollar and euro, although its share is low compared with the two major currencies, which account for 90% of all holdings. Important also for foreign investors is the Bank of Japan's stance on currency management: there is no regular intervention in the market although one-off intervention in a crisis might be possible.
- *Japanese wealth held abroad,* estimated at $5–6 trillion (private and public sector combined): this has been fed by large annual capital outflows. These external funds play an important part in both Japan's wealth management and in global financial markets, implying that Japanese investment decisions may be a critical factor in some trades, especially in high-yield currencies. However, this large pool of foreign assets could play a greater role in enhancing Tokyo's position as an international financial centre.

There are also concerns, in particular the potential for foreign support for the stock market to weaken in the long run and the low level of foreign interest in other parts of the Japanese financial system. Future strength may require increased foreign participation in the bond market, to create a more international market and enhance Tokyo's opportunities in Asian debt markets. A shift in household wealth from bank deposits to managed funds would also enhance business in the financial services sector and improve Japan's asset demand/supply balance but a speedy and substantial transfer looks unlikely after the experience of the 2008–09 global crisis. Although the government is keen to encourage such transfers it is not clear what incentives (such as tax breaks or capital guarantees) it is able to offer. Another means of tackling this issue may be to look for change within the banks themselves.

The impact of large speculative capital flows on currency volatility and investment returns also needs to be addressed, for example, by encouraging long-term investment of Japan's foreign asset base, which could also benefit Tokyo's status as an international financial centre. This would be consistent with moves to expand banks' operations abroad.

17 The shares in world capitalization vary considerably from year to year, the recent average being about 8%.

4. Long-run Risk to the Stock Market?

Figure 13: Stock market price/earning ratio

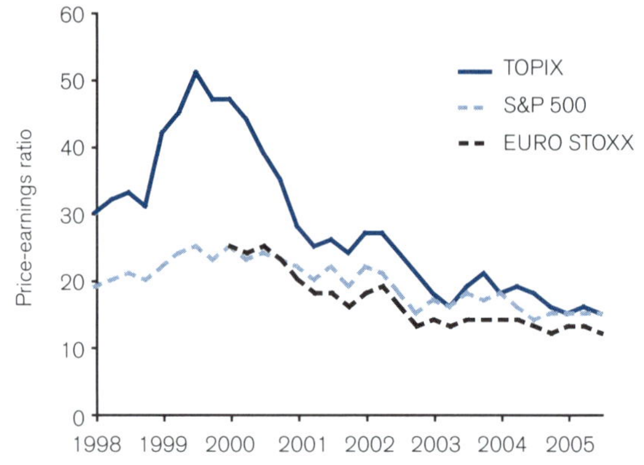

Note: 12-month forward EPS is used to calculate PER ratio.
Source: I/B/E/S

While the relatively high stock market capitalization plays an important supporting role for Tokyo as a financial centre, there is concern that such support could diminish over time. This high market capitalization has been based not only on substantial corporate earnings (profits), which are typically strongly correlated with national GDP over the medium to long run, but also on historically high price/earnings ratios (PER) for Japanese equities. Both of these determinants could be vulnerable in the future: company earnings growth may be dampened by weak economic growth and high taxes, while the PER premium could decline.

Although the PER has fallen sharply since the bubble years, when it reached stunningly unsustainable peaks of around 60–70, it has remained somewhat elevated compared with other major markets. Given the turmoil in global markets and economies over the last year, and continuing difficulties with recession and financial restructuring, current market data are particularly difficult to assess and comparisons may be distorted. According to quoted figures,[18] the current PER for the Japanese market has been trading in the 10–15 range, closely in line with the US market (in the 10–11 range) but still several points higher than many other leading markets (presently trading as low as 7–9 given concerns over the weakening profits outlook). A relatively high PER need not signify mispricing or overvaluation – there may be strong justifications for Japanese listed companies enjoying higher ratings than average – but it inevitably raises a question over sustainability and the fear for a further downward correction in the market.

In summary, there are three key causes for concern over the long-run trend for the Japanese stock market:

- The PER could continue on a downward trend, dragging the stock market valuation back to well below 100% of GDP and downgrading Japan's rank in terms of its share of global equities.
- Even assuming the PER represents fair value and remains stable, relatively low earnings growth could also weaken Japan's stock market valuation compared with the rest of the world. Company earnings tend to grow roughly in line with GDP, so Japan's weak economic growth prospects will lead to a trend decline not only in Japan's share of world GDP but also in its share of global corporate profits and the global equity market (evidence of the correlation in shares is shown in Figure 14).
- If slow growth in the economy and stock market implies that Japanese equities will under-perform relative to other world markets over the long run, this will further reduce the market's appeal, especially for foreign investors, which could generate not just a gradual downgrading but a rapid and substantial exodus of funds.

18 For example, *Financial Times* daily market reports, January 2009.

Figure 14: Correlation of GDP and market capitalization shares (with and without the US)

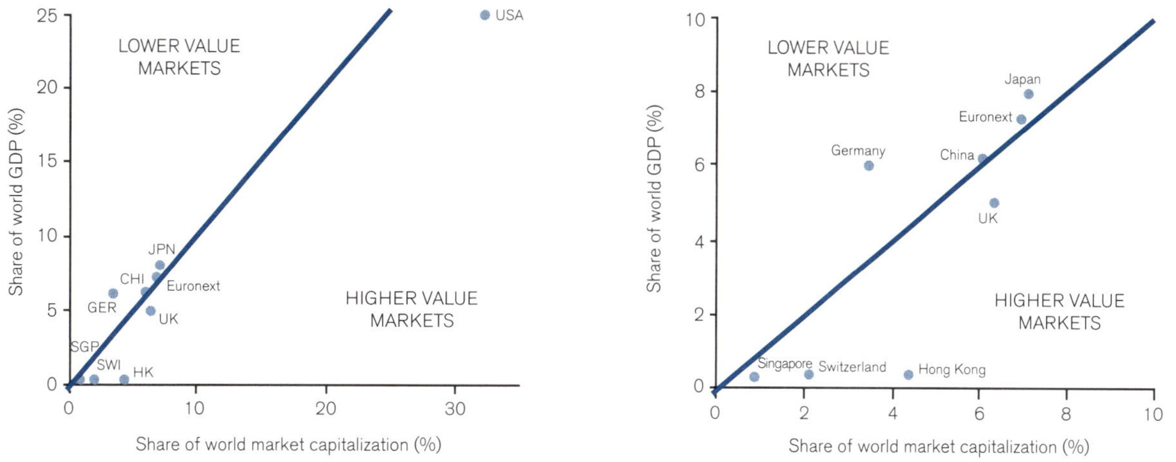

Sources: WFE, UN

In the face of slow national economic growth, the way to secure a continued high stock market valuation and ranking is for listed companies to target earnings growth well in excess of national nominal GDP growth. For example, Japanese companies may aggressively expand their businesses into high-growth sectors and/or into Asian and global markets, not relying on growth in their domestic market alone and leaving low-margin business to non-listed companies, the public sector and/or foreign companies. This is tough but feasible. In fact, there are already a number of large, world-class Japanese companies that have demonstrated their ability to compete and grow on a global basis. The Swiss stock market also provides an example of the 'headquartering' effect, enabling a global corporate sector and a relatively highly rated stock market to survive in spite of a small, low-growth home economy (as shown in the entry for Switzerland in Figure 14). Hong Kong provides an even more extreme example of a market capitalization greatly exceeding its home GDP base (also shown in Figure 14) although this may be considered atypical given its links to China.

Figure 15: Comparison of corporate tax rates

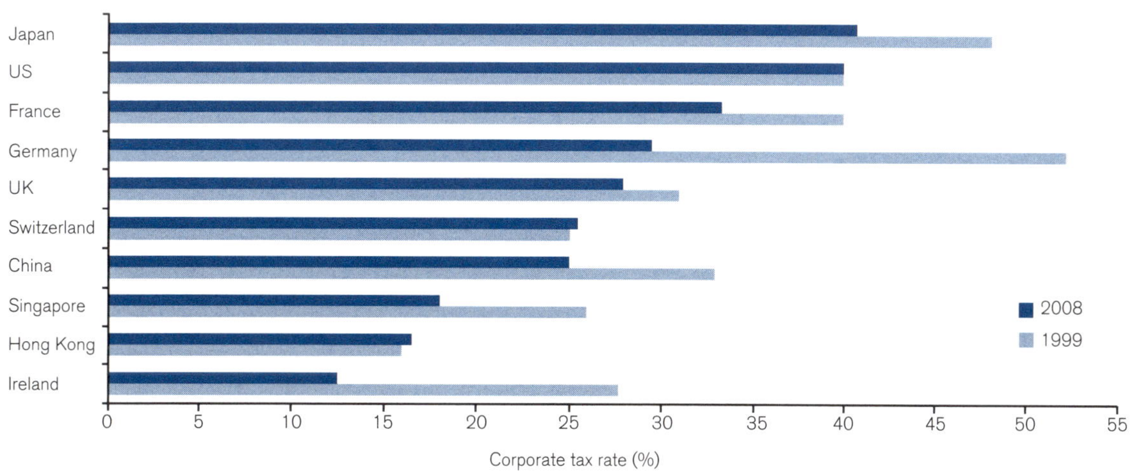

Source: KPMG

However, it does pose a considerable challenge for the corporate sector to sustain rapid global expansion over the long run with diminishing support from the home market – and, as mentioned already, it creates exposure to uncontrollable external risks, such as that posed by the current global recession. Sustaining high trend growth in corporate earnings may also require changes in government policy to encourage global companies to remain headquartered in Japan given international competition for the status of 'host' country – for example, tax policies may have to adapt. In this regard, Japan has been less keen to follow the international trend towards lower corporate tax rates over the present decade. Its current rate (40.69%) is higher than any other OECD country in addition to its main competitors in the Asia-Pacific region, notably Singapore and Hong Kong where rates are less than half those in Japan. Further competition may even widen this gap.

If the long-run threat to corporate growth is not successfully addressed, the obvious risk is that the stock market will gradually slip down the global rankings and Tokyo will be unable to rely on rising equity values and a highly rated stock market to maintain its top ranking as a financial centre. Even more importantly, Japan's economy may be affected by corporate flight and a further hollowing out of the industrial base.

5. Support for Tokyo from Other Markets

With the stock market's position at risk over the medium to long term, what support is there for Tokyo as a financial centre from Japan's status in other markets and services?

The bond market epitomizes Japan's problem in acting as an international financial centre – it meets the criterion of being a large, mature, open market, representing 15% of the global bond market (greater than Japan's share in the global equity market), yet foreign investments have struggled to reach 6–7% of this market.

This has not posed a funding problem because Japan has not needed to attract foreign investors to support the market, thanks to its large domestic pool of risk-averse investors and persistently large current account balances, representing surplus net national savings. Such financial self-sufficiency and demand for bonds has advantages, for example keeping local interest rates low in spite of the high level of government debt. Arguably, demand for 'safe' government debt in Japan is even higher than the seemingly ample supply based on the high price for this asset class (i.e. Japan's remarkably low yields). But there is also a cost attached to low yields in terms of Japan's isolation from international markets and thus lack of support for Tokyo as a financial centre.

Strong domestic demand for very conservative savings vehicles in the home economy has kept bond yields very low, even in the face of persistently large public-sector deficits and continuing increases in debt – a trend that is not expected to do more than modestly reverse given the intractable problems surrounding imposition of tax increases or cuts in spending. The annual deficit that has to be funded is likely to reach $500 billion in the next few years and overall debt turnover may be twice this figure. Government debt (gross) has now risen to 160–170% of GDP (the net position is somewhat better but still high at around 100% of GDP), yet 10-year benchmark bonds have typically traded at yields of just 1–1.5% over the last 15 years. Institutionalized 'home bias' and conservative investment patterns have kept some $8–9 trillion of Japanese savings locked into domestic bonds.

Figure 16: Holdings of Japanese bonds by foreign investors

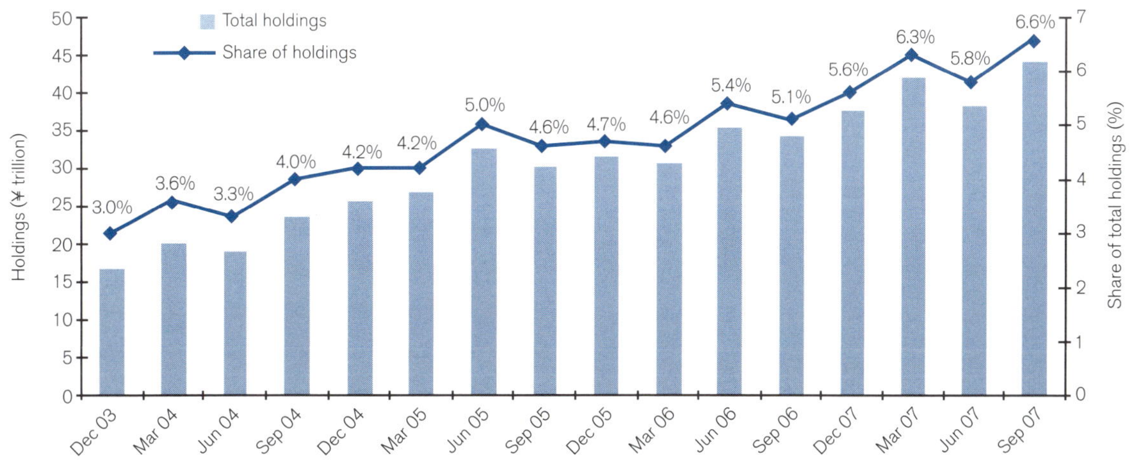

Source: Bank of Japan

Low yields have made debt appear more 'affordable' for the government compared with the competitive rates required for attracting foreign investors, which would probably have been at least double the yields actually seen in recent years. The government has approximately halved its interest costs on debt – a saving of perhaps $100 billion in 2008, or 2% of GDP, money which would otherwise have gone mostly into interest income for Japanese savers and pensioners. Arguably, this could have provided a stimulus to the economy at the same time as encouraging foreign investor interest.

The share of foreign investors has actually risen steadily into the 6–7% range from an even more meagre 3–3.5% in 2003 but it will have to rise even further before the market can be considered truly international. Foreign investors represent some 25% of the US bond market and as much as 50% of the government market, for example. And foreign investment in Japan's smaller stock market totals around $1–1.5 trillion, about double the investment in bonds. If bonds were to attract simply the same sums as equities, this would roughly double the foreign share of the market to 10–15% and significantly increase the presence of foreign investors in Tokyo. A fairer share of the bond market might arguably be much higher than this, of course, perhaps around 25–30% or $2.5–3 trillion.

Figure 17: Potential growth in foreign investment in Japanese markets

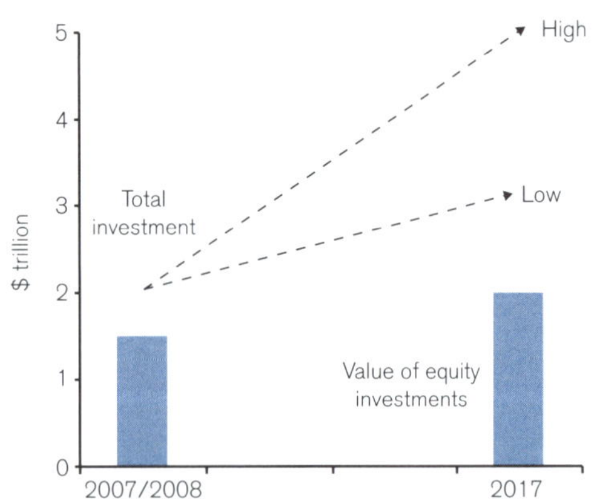

High estimate: bond holdings rise to match equity stakes
Low estimate: no increase in holdings except for equity investments

Sources: WFE, ISFL

For such a large bond market, unique in Asia, Japan is currently under-performing relative to its potential to attract foreign investors and also to serve a wider function, for example, as the Asian counterpart to the US and Europe in a better-balanced tripartite bond world.

Table 8: Evidence of converging bond yields

10yr yields	2007 Q1	2008 Q1	2009 Jan
Japan	1.7	1.3	1.2
US	4.7	3.7	2.3
Germany	4.0	4.0	3.0
UK	4.9	4.4	3.4

Source: *Financial Times*

This situation could change markedly in 2009 owing to the startling impact of the economic and financial crisis. US and EU government bond yields have tumbled as official short-term interest rates have plunged and concern over inflation has turned into fear of deflation amidst a deep and possibly prolonged economic recession. This means that key global yields have moved closer towards low Japanese levels. Indeed, yields may possibly converge further during 2009, making Japanese bonds more attractive to foreign as well as domestic investors.

Of course, part of this convergence in yields is cyclical and thus temporary. However, given the experience of the crisis, the likely persistence of lower growth rates and inflation and population ageing, it is possible that US and EU bonds will remain closer to low Japanese yields in the future. The generally declining trend in yields over the last decade also suggests that differentials could narrow.[19]

The perception of Japan as a stable 'safe haven' for cautious investors has also been boosted by the rise of the yen (up by about 15% against the dollar and 30% against the euro by year-end 2008) and the global surge in risk aversion – as illustrated by the sharp rise in emerging-market risk premiums and widening market spreads across European markets, where investors have become wary of the implications of bulging fiscal deficits and debt (coupled, in some cases, with outbreaks of social unrest and rising political risk).

19 Arguments in this respect are provided in Paola Subacchi and Vanessa Rossi, *Thinking Longer, Working Harder: How Long-dated Bonds Can Help Europe's Ageing Population*, Chatham House Briefing Paper IEP BP 06/01, February 2006.

While Japan's fiscal position and the scale of its government debt had seemed troubling in the past, they now appear less of a deterrent to investors. Indeed, overturning orthodox assessments of the risk posed by high debt/GDP ratios, Japan could serve as an example of how conservatively run countries with ageing populations and substantial domestic savings can safely expand government debt at low interest rates without endangering stability. The debt simply reflects demand for secure investment vehicles: inelastic demand implies bond holdings are relatively insensitive to low rates of return.

A reversal in foreign-investor interest in the relatively unpopular Japanese bond market would certainly indicate a significant change of view. Recent recommendations regarding the development of Japanese financial services and policies to support market growth would need to be reviewed and the bond market might feature both differently and more prominently than before. New-found interest would also be very beneficial for the position of Japan as an international centre – a general surge in investor interest in secure bonds could make Japan the leader in this sector in Asia, playing to its unrivalled position in Asian bond markets.

While most of the focus of previous reports and recommendations has been corporate growth and the stock market, with high government debt seen as a burden for the economy and the tax outlook, a new look at the bond market may be in order. Examined in a new light, this large, mature market may be a surprising benefit for the financial sector and economy. But, after all, the scale of the global crisis has made the unthinkable both thinkable and do-able. This may be just another aspect of the unexpected changes brought about by the crash of 2008.

6. Japan's Banking System after the 2008 Crisis

Table 9: Largest Japanese financial companies by market value, 2008

		Industry (world rank)	Market value ($m)
1	Mitsubishi UFJ Financial	Banking (10)	93,846.4
2	Sumitomo Mitsui Financial	Banking (31)	50,969.7
3	Mizuho Financial	Banking (40)	41,790.6
4	Millea Holdings	Insurance (10)	29,744.8
5	Nomura Holdings	Financial (8)	29,429.0
6	Resona	Banking	19,011.7
7	Mitsui Sumitomo Insurance	Insurance	15,308.9
8	T & D Holdings	Insurance	12,918.5
9	Orix	Financial	12,596.1
10	Dalwa Securities Group	Financial	12,193.0

Source: FT Japan 500 2008

The global financial crisis has not only served to make Japan's bond market surprisingly more competitive than it was *vis-à-vis* other major markets, it has also revealed the relative strength of Japanese banks compared with equivalent US and European banks. In this sense, Japan appears to be a relative winner: so far, its financial system has weathered the global crisis in better shape than the world's leaders (albeit not entirely unscathed, as indicated by current moves to raise capital in response to the losses in the existing capital base caused by falling stock markets).

The very large base of low-cost bank deposits in Japan (almost as large as that in the US) has provided liquidity and support in the context of a global credit crunch that has badly exposed those banks most reliant on interbank lending. However, like other countries, Japan is expected to suffer substantial losses in the corporate sector, raising concern over the impact of the global recession on corporate debt, increasing non-performing loans, defaults and subsequent write-offs in the banking sector.

Figure 18: Market value losses by major financial companies, 2006–08

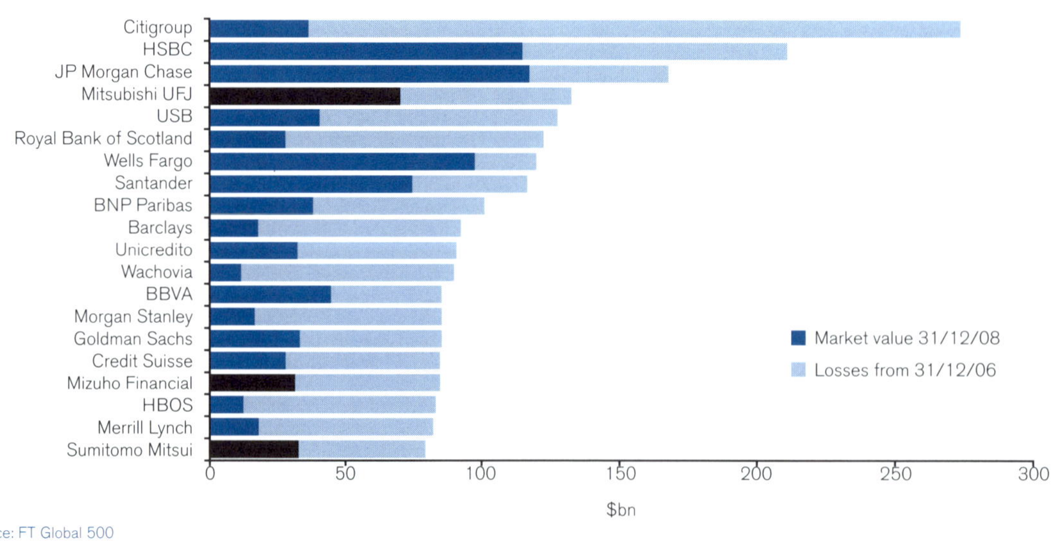

Source: FT Global 500

Table 10: Reported non-performing loans (NPLs)

All Banks (¥ tn)	Sept-1999	Sept-2000	Sept-2001	Sept-2002	Sept-2003	Sept-2004	Sept-2005	Sept-2006	Sept-2007	Sept-2008
Total loans	532.8	531.8	526.1	485.6	462.3	449.5	450.0	463.2	475.2	489.0
NPLs	31.3	32.9	36.8	40.1	31.6	23.8	15.9	12.3	11.9	12.3
%	5.9	6.2	7.0	8.3	6.8	5.3	3.5	2.7	2.5	2.5

Source: JFSA

Table 11: Bank deposits (Q2 2008)

	$ billion
US	11,165
Japan	**9,163**
UK	4,468
Germany	4,248
France	2,308
Italy	1,694
Switzerland	693

Source: IFS

The relative robustness of the Japanese banking sector in the face of the global storm is in part due to its fortuitous preoccupation with its own restructuring and recovery from the prolonged crisis of the 1990s. As noted earlier, the Japanese banks had already raised capital adequacy, written off bad debts and were just beginning to re-emerge from the long period of recovery as problems in the US and Europe began to appear in 2007.

In addition, they mostly avoided involvement in the markets that have caused the greatest damage in the banking sector – that is, US and EU collateralized debt instruments and structured products, including mortgage-backed securities linked to the US sub-prime market. Having suffered for so long from the problems caused by their own domestic property sector, the Japanese banks were probably disinclined to become involved in this sector abroad, although they had started to step up purchases of foreign assets in their balance sheets between 2005 and early 2008. This activity may have led to losses on these portfolios in local currency terms, if only because the yen picked up strongly in 2008.

Figure 19: Biggest sub-prime losses

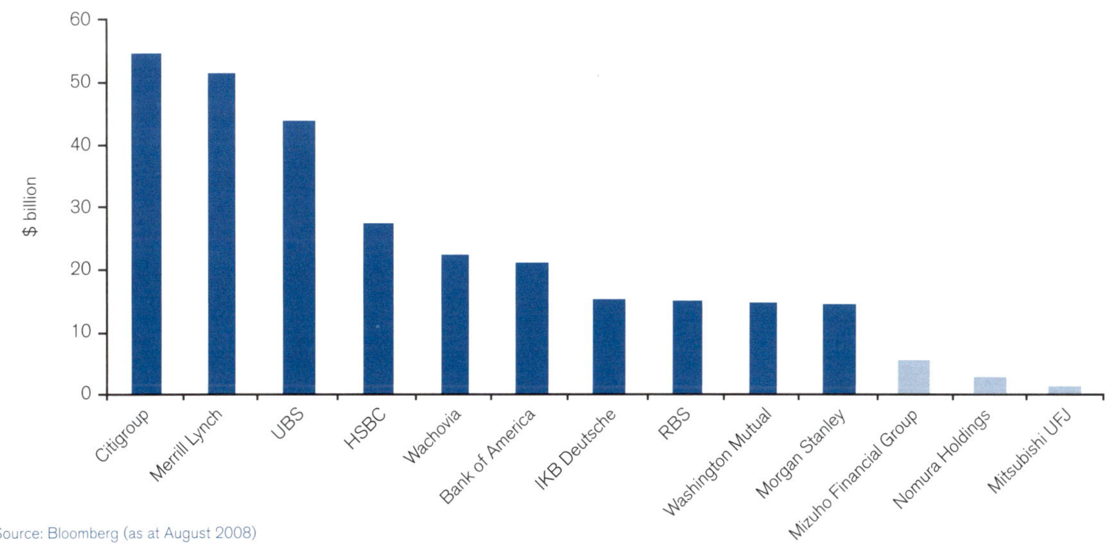

Source: Bloomberg (as at August 2008)

Although Japan cannot avoid losses, they will be less severe than in the US and Europe. In addition, it has learnt the lessons of the 1990s, and now has considerable experience of handling such situations effectively and swiftly.

New opportunities for Japan's banks?

The change in fortunes across the global banking system means that Tokyo has been given an unexpected opportunity to regain some of its former momentum and to take new initiatives in global finance, such as expanding operations abroad through M&A opportunities in a distressed global financial sector. Nomura's purchase of parts of Lehman Brothers' operations and investments by Mitsubishi UFJ are two examples already mentioned.

Although recent action has been within the banking sector, there may be scope for new ventures in other areas such as fund management and insurance as well, extending Tokyo's involvement in a broader spectrum of global financial services and capitalizing on the perception that Japan can maintain a relatively stable, conservatively run financial sector. However, to succeed, such trends must be backed up by favourable opinion and supportive policies in Japan. In this context, what backing is the government providing for Tokyo's position as an international centre for finance?

Policy-makers have been actively examining ways of encouraging growth in both the corporate sector and the financial services industry, which are seen as crucial in supporting the future investment and economic growth outlook. Following extensive reviews and consultations, various policy changes have been recommended and enacted, chiefly focusing on issues of the regulatory environment and access to international professional expertise that are typically quoted as damaging to Japan's international standing in financial market surveys and investment reports. Reviews of tax reform[20] have also highlighted the need to cut taxes but typically also express concern that persistently large public-sector deficits make it difficult to reduce the high tax burden without other offsetting policy adjustments.

Overall, the policy stance will remain favourable to changes that increase support for Japan's company finances and improve the long-run performance of the economy. The current crisis will tend to reinforce this stance. But it will also add a greater sense of urgency, given the immediate need for financial support for the corporate sector and economy to help moderate the impact of the global recession and strengthen the chances of a rapid recovery as global demand picks up again.

Japan's economy has been hit exceptionally hard through its exposure to the massive downturn in global demand for cars, consumer electronics and investment equipment. Japan's manufacturers are world leaders – innovative and competitive – but they are also highly

Table 12: Timeline of major bank rescues

'Rescuer'	Country	Date	'Rescued'	Country
Bank of America	US	15-Sep-08	Merrill Lynch	US
Mitsubishi UFJ	Japan	22-Sep-08	Morgan Stanley	US
Nomura	Japan	23-Sep-08	Lehman Brothers	US
JP Morgan Chase*	US	25-Sep-08	Washington Mutual	US
Wells Fargo	US	03-Oct-08	Wachovia	US
Swiss govt, QIA	Swiss, Qatar	16-Oct-08	UBS	Swiss
Central Bank of Libya	Libya	17-Oct-08	Unicredit	Italy
QIA Challenger and Abu Dhabi	Gulf	31-Oct-08	Barclays	UK

* Also 'rescued' Bear Stearns in March 2008.

Source: Various news reports

20 For example OECD, 'Reforming the Tax System in Japan to Promote Fiscal Sustainability and Economic Growth', Economics Department Working Papers No. 650.

vulnerable to this extraordinary global cycle. This implies that they need the support of a 'sympathetic' business and financial environment to survive and prosper. The liquid domestic banking sector is well placed to play a key role in helping companies, and the economy, through the crisis to recovery. Stock markets cannot easily be used for fundraising in current crisis conditions. Arguably, they are better suited to being the prime source of funding for high-growth or stable non-cyclical sectors than for highly cyclical sectors, as equity investors may be less supportive of cyclical sectors in severe downturns than a relationship-oriented domestic banking system.

Japanese banks will inevitably be called on to play a critical role in both managing investment abroad and providing support for Japan's corporate sector. In the long run, it may be possible to encourage a more active role in markets for Japan's household savings given the extremely high share of wealth (over 50%) held in bank deposits. But in the current climate, extremely risk-averse investors are even less likely to move out of the safety of deposits. Relationship banking will continue to be important in enabling Japan's corporate sector to thrive, maintaining long-run growth objectives and investments even in the face of this major recession.

In addition, the banks can help improve the management of Japanese wealth abroad through growth in their international business; like the global manufacturers, they can expand abroad to generate higher levels of business activity and raise profitability. The low-cost deposit base in 'savings-heavy' Japan can be used to develop business in other markets that offer a high nominal growth environment and thus higher profit margins.

In the present credit crunch, Japanese banks can use their low-cost funds to raise market share in higher margin business in 'savings-lite' countries. Unlike short-termist carry trade, which has the potential to cause excessive volatility in the yen as well as in recipient-country financial markets and Japanese investors' returns, such investments meet the criteria of being more stable and more strategic.

The international expansion of the banks and other financial institutions would offer Japan a more structured and strategic way of investing in foreign assets than focusing on short-term trading activity in the markets. Organic growth means gradually developing this business to earn better margins and fee income, whereas acquisitions could provide a more rapid advance. With asset prices in the financial sector currently severely depressed, there are clearly opportunities for strong institutions to step in and more aggressively expand business in the financial sector.

7. Market Survey Results and Competitiveness Indicators

Apart from examining background support for the scale of Japan's financial markets and Tokyo's importance in the world system, there are many other factors that determine the success and growth of financial centres – from ability to innovate and transact efficiently, to access to professional staff and the cost of living. One way of encapsulating such views is to draw on the material provide by timely and comprehensive surveys of the financial sector worldwide. How do these view Japan and Tokyo?

Comparative performance of international financial centres

As mentioned in Chapter 1, Tokyo is ranked among the top ten international financial centres according to recent reports by the City of London and the World Economic Forum. (The latter addresses the overall national financial sector, although this distinction is less relevant for countries with one dominant centre such as Japan.) Although both reports reaffirmed the dominance of London and New York as the world's two truly *global* financial centres,[21] Tokyo's position in the world and in Asia is much more contentious, especially as each report has a distinct focus – the City of London on financial competitiveness, and the WEF on financial development.

In terms of international comparisons, it is clear that Tokyo, Hong Kong and Singapore are all jostling for position as the premier centre in Asia. But whereas the City of London survey places Tokyo behind its two major Asian rivals (which themselves trail only London and New York), the WEF ranks Japan solidly ahead of either. This is largely due to the greater weight placed on Japan's large, developed economy and financial system (particularly its highly efficient banks), strong financial intermediary skills, financial stability and an overall well-rounded performance across most categories considered. In contrast, the City of London's assessments give greater emphasis to the general competitiveness of each city as viewed from the perspective of those who directly participate in its financial markets. Despite the lower position of Tokyo relative to its Asian competitors, the City of London notes Tokyo's improvement in the rankings (overtaking Chicago and Frankfurt since the previous survey six months earlier), as well as in various specific categories such as market access, infrastructure and general competitiveness. Like the WEF, the City of London also highlights the strength of the Japanese economy and its high stock market capitalization.

Table 13: Asia/Pacific/Middle East rankings (world rankings in brackets)

	GFCI4		WEF
1	Singapore (3)	1	**Japan (4)**
2	Hong Kong (4)	2	Hong Kong (8)
3	**Tokyo (7)**	3	Singapore (10)
4	Sydney (10)	4	Australia (11)
5	Dubai (23)	5	United Arab Emirates (16)
6	Melbourne (27)	6	Korea, Republic (19)
7	Shanghai (34)	7	Malaysia (20)
8	Bahrain (43)	8	Kuwait (26)
9	Qatar (45)	9	Saudi Arabia (27)
10	Beijing (47)	10	Bahrain (28)

Sources: City of London, WEF

Both reports make largely the same criticisms, which are mainly related to corporate governance, high corporate tax rates, and long-term legal and regulatory issues. It should be

21 A *global* financial centre may be defined as one whose institutions have a global reach in the broadest possible range of financial operations. Most centres, however, can be said to be *international* owing to their connectedness with international markets to a greater or lesser degree.

noted, however, that the latter are far from unique to Japan, particularly in the context of current financial problems (the City of London report, for example, already makes note of the negative effects of the credit crunch on the perceptions of regulation for New York and London, the latter mostly as a result of the Northern Rock affair). Other weaknesses mentioned include poor access to international financial personnel, Japan's large public debt, and the difficulty in accessing private credit, loans and venture capital (compared with the relative ease of entry into local equity markets).

The fact that the Asia-Pacific region is no longer dominated by a single financial centre prompts a more detailed comparison of Tokyo with its regional rivals. According to the City of London, Hong Kong and Singapore rank within the top ten in all sub-indices for industry sectors and areas of competitiveness, and are positioned higher than Tokyo in each one as well. According to the WEF, Hong Kong's strengths lie in its institutional environment, particularly in legal and regulation issues, a non-distortionary tax regime, high-quality infrastructure and large banking system, as well as access to different forms of capital. On the other hand, its main weakness is seen as the quality of its human capital. Meanwhile, Singapore rates highly on account of its strong institutional and business environment, the lowest regulatory burden among countries listed, legal effectiveness, and financial stability. Concern is mostly raised on account of its inefficient banking system.

The importance of survey methodologies in determining rankings

It is important to note the reasons why the rankings in the City of London and WEF reports differ. As mentioned previously, the GFCI4 is based on individual assessments by market participants (supported by a predictive model to estimate individual responses to questionnaires for centres with which the participants were not familiar) combined with instrumental factors based on external indices. As such, its overall rankings are seen as a reflection of sector results and of the way each of these sectors is viewed in terms of its importance by participants.

It therefore comes as no surprise that Tokyo's position suffers on account of its business environment (a category that includes taxation and regulation), an area in which it markedly under-performs, as survey respondents consider this the key area of competitiveness.

In contrast, the WEF report gives added consideration to the degree of development of the financial sector and its intermediaries, categories in which Tokyo is well positioned. It also sources its indicators by either external data or surveys, but not both. With this distinction in mind, it is interesting to note that Japan's weakest indicators were predominantly obtained from surveys. Assuming a generally poorer perception of Japanese financial markets by survey respondents, it would therefore be reasonable to conclude that the GFCI4's instrumental factors may be negatively affected by the use of survey results for each indicator, with the result that Tokyo is slightly brought down in rankings compared with the WEF.

Ultimately it must be emphasized that, despite similar indicators and conclusions, the City of London clearly ranks financial centres 'in terms of *competitiveness*' whereas the WEF report focuses on the '*development* of the world's financial systems'. This is an important distinction which should serve to preclude any premature conclusions regarding the position of Tokyo as an international financial centre on the basis of any one particular report. It should also be apparent that the City of London ranks individual centres, whereas the WEF deals with countries as a whole. This could lead to comparison difficulties in countries with multiple major centres (the United States, Switzerland), although this is not likely to be the case in Japan given the low ranking of the only other centre mentioned (Osaka) in the GFCI4. Results for both reports should thus be fairly comparable, suggesting that it is not unreasonable to see Tokyo and Japan as synonymous; there are no substantive issues of competitiveness between Japanese centres.

Cost-competitiveness indicators

Although not directly touched upon by either of the reports discussed above, various economic and social indicators could have an additional effect on the perception of Tokyo as a competitive international finance centre,

Figure 20: Relation between average monthly wages ($) and value of the yen

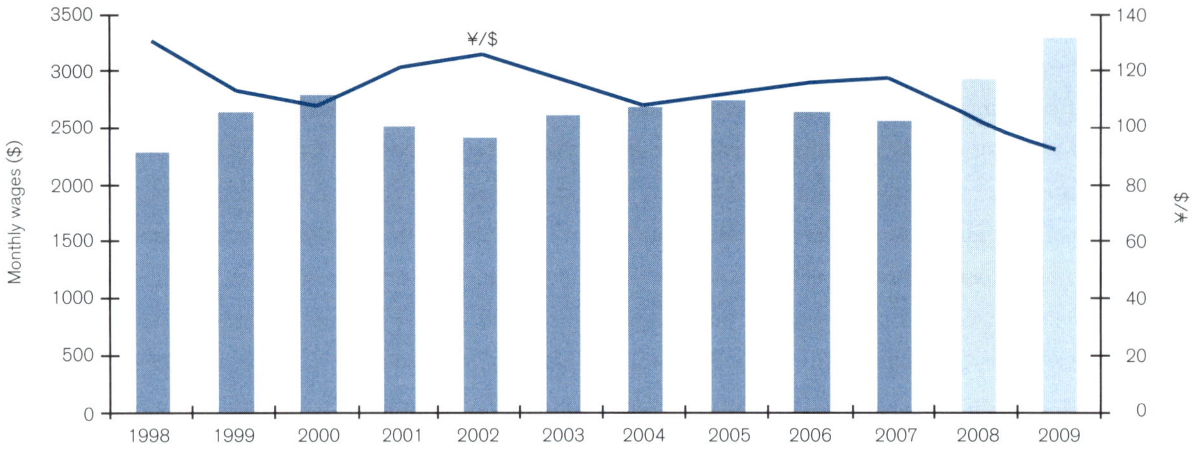

Note: ¥/$ for 2009 and monthly wages for 2008-09 are estimates.
Sources: ILO, Oanda

including traditional measures of competitiveness for economies (wages and costs) and subjective views of the attractions of various cities/countries as places to live and work (access to housing, transport, schools etc.).

One of the more obvious economic indicators is the level of wages and rates relative to other countries (Figure 20). In dollar terms, fluctuations in Japanese wages show a pronounced (inverse) correlation with the strength of the yen. This suggests that swings in the yen are the key variant in determining changes in international wage competitiveness as Japan's domestic wage growth (in yen) has been and remains both stable and very weak.

However, there are both positive and negative effects of wages that affect what is meant by the 'competitiveness' of rival international financial centres. On the one hand, finance as a high-value activity is undoubtedly attracted to centres which can provide high salaries and bonuses for professionals. On the other, high basic staff and living costs may be a disincentive for foreign business. In both of these respects Japan performs less than optimally: incentive-based compensation is ranked very low in the WEF report, and the recent sharp appreciation of the yen (against the US dollar and therefore against Hong Kong and Singapore – with an even more pronounced move against the UK pound) is expected to raise average wages and the cost of living relative to other international centres.

A similar 'soft' indicator of international competitiveness is the cost of living in each financial centre. According to Mercer's annual Cost of Living surveys (Figure 21), Tokyo remained the most expensive of the three major Asian financial centres in 2008 but less so than in previous years (all three cities are, today, more expensive than the baseline, New York). However, this situation may also change owing to the strengthening of the yen which is likely to push Tokyo well ahead of its two Asian rivals in 2009.

Figure 21: Cost of living in Asia

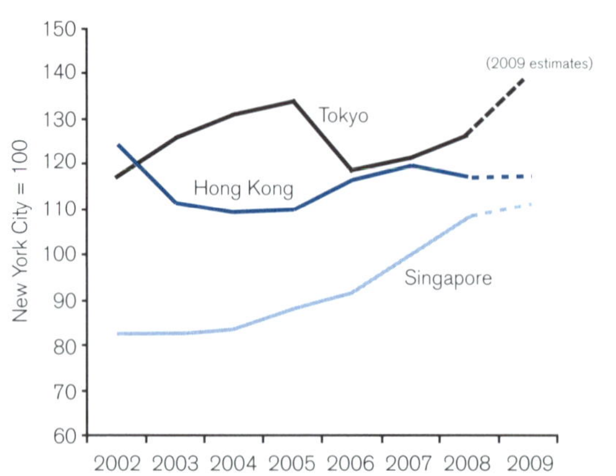

Source: Mercer

Summary of key points

The City of London and WEF reports both point to the high ranking of Tokyo alongside the world's major financial centres such as London and New York as well as the Asian centres of Hong Kong and Singapore. The methodology and emphasis in the WEF report tend to produce a ranking more precisely correlated with Japan's economic position in the world and the overall development of its financial markets. On the other hand, market participant opinion, as exemplified by the City of London report, has Tokyo trailing slightly behind. This assessment is based on qualitative arguments, essentially giving the impression that Japan requires further changes in its institutional arrangements, particularly in the areas of taxation and regulation, in order to encourage financial businesses to expand in Tokyo.

Forthcoming updates of the surveys will illustrate how far the new measures taken by the Japanese Financial Services Agency (JFSA) have allayed the concerns of participants and also whether the global crisis has significantly affected relative scores of the financial centres.

Along with the additional indicators presented here, which point to a new deterioration in Japan's cost-competitiveness, the rankings provide valuable insights regarding the strengths and weaknesses of Tokyo's financial markets. However, any conclusions need to take into account the particular caveats and methodological discrepancies in these surveys.

Broadly speaking, there is a common theme to the reported disadvantages of Tokyo, based on issues such as corporate taxes, regulations and business environment, but some criticisms are also somewhat vague and subjective, including complaints about 'soft' indicators ranging from various aspects of the cost of living to inconvenience in terms of flights and connections elsewhere in Asia and working conditions. Although it may be difficult to treat the more nebulous complaints about the conditions in Tokyo, the more concrete points that can be addressed by government are receiving attention. Policy initiatives are reviewed in the next chapter.

8. Government Policy

With the aim of addressing many of the perceived shortcomings of Japan's financial sector, the Japanese Financial Services Agency announced a concrete policy package entitled 'Strengthening the Competitiveness of Japan's Financial and Capital Markets' in December 2007. The key proposals in terms of changes in regulations and business environment were implemented speedily by the JFSA in 2008 and are most likely responsible for at least some of the improvements in Japan's position shown in market surveys conducted during the course of that year. Furthermore, it is understood that for Japan to sustain economic growth given its declining and rapidly ageing population, there is an urgent need to strengthen the competitiveness of its financial and capital markets in order to enable companies to raise capital and investment for the future. This applies as much to the many small and medium-sized enterprises as it does to large corporations.

The plan also recognized that global competition among New York, London, Hong Kong, Singapore and other markets has intensified during the period when Japan was involved in resolving the problems brought about by the collapse of the bubble economy and subsequent restructuring. While focusing on these problems, Japan has fallen behind its rivals.

In the opinion of the JFSA, Japan's advantages lie in having a large economy and substantial wealth, highlighting household financial assets worth around $15 trillion (based on data from September 2008). Japan also has a strong, technologically advanced manufacturing base, and geographically it is part of Asia, the world's most dynamic regional economy. It is well positioned to take part in raising capital to meet the investment needs of emerging Asia. In terms of infrastructure, Japan maintains a stable legal framework, a well-educated labour force, good public safety and an efficient transport system.

However, the following three weaknesses are identified:

- Shortages of skilled professionals in certain disciplines, such as financial engineering, law and accounting, and especially in areas requiring both English proficiency and professional competence in finance and other related fields. An often quoted reflection of this shortage is the lack of hedge funds and the talented professionals that they generally attract.
- The legacy of the bubble collapse and the prolonged restructuring process, which has cast a long shadow over the performance and competitive position of Japan's financial sector.[22]
- The maintenance of large bank deposits by risk-averse households: this puts too much onus on banks acting as intermediaries for most transactions and investments in Japan, implying that too much liquidity and risk are managed through the banking system rather than through professional investment management. This problem is compounded by the limited diversity of financial products available.

The way in which Japan's household savings are bottled up in low-interest deposit accounts contrasts starkly with the United States, where households keep little cash in deposit accounts and keep a very large share of their wealth in the stock market. Japan's deposit base is 80% of the US base and double that of Germany. Notably, the proportions held in insurance and pensions are about the same in Japan and the US.

22 The global crisis and currently challenging conditions could not have been anticipated when the JFSA proposals were released.

Table 14: Financial assets held by households (September 2008)

	Deposits and Currency	Bonds	Investment Trusts	Shares and equities	Insurance and pension reserves
Japan	53.1%	2.9%	4.0%	8.1%	27.4%
US	13.5%	8.7%	12.5%	33.1%	28.4%

Source: Japan FSA

Policy recommendations supportive

The JFSA's plan for strengthening the competitiveness of Japan's financial markets is aimed at broadening the investment opportunities to be offered to households in order to reduce the share of wealth held in bank deposits and limit the role played by the banks as financial intermediaries. Owing to the large amount of liquidity in Japan, Japanese markets can contribute to both domestic and foreign (especially Asian) countries' economic growth by supplying companies with capital. It is recognized that Japan's financial and capital markets must be able to serve the diverse needs of both domestic and foreign investors and borrowers. The financial services industry should generate high added value, thereby contributing to sustainable economic growth and high-quality job opportunities.

The JFSA plan establishes four major measures:

- *Creating reliable and vibrant markets* by providing various opportunities for raising investment and capital. This involves introducing a highly flexible market designed for professional investors based on the principle of self-responsibility (such as the Alternative Investment Market in London[23]), expanding the scope of securities for which disclosure in English is permitted, diversification of exchange-traded funds (ETFs), and the establishment of a framework for ETFs alliances between stock and commodity exchanges.
- *Revitalizing the financial services industry and promoting competition.* Key points include the relaxing of firewall regulations, lifting the ban on interlocking officers and employees among banking, securities and insurance businesses in a financial

Table 15: Timeline of financial policies adopted

1	'Financial Big Bang' (commission fees, partial removal of firewalls, liberalization of foreign exchange transactions)	1996–2000s
2	Formation of 3 mega financial holding companies through mergers	1996–1997
3	Adoption of the current value accounting system	1997–2005
4	Establishment of single regulator system (FSA) similar to the UK's	1998–2000
5	Continuous convergence of accounting standards (Japanese GAAS) with IFRS	
6	FSA announces *Plan for Strengthening the Competitiveness of Japan's Financial and Capital Markets*	Dec 2007
7	Shift from rule-based (US) to principle-based (UK) regulation	Apr 2008
8	J-SOX Law on financial disclosure of listed firms	Apr 2008
9	Increased variety of financial assets (ETF, JDR)	
10	Greater cooperation with foreign exchanges	
11	Revised financial instrument and exchange law	Jun 2008
12	Discussion on the removal of firewalls	Jun 2009

Source: Prof. Sayuri Shirai, Keio University

23 There is a planned joint venture between the London Stock Exchange and Tokyo on setting up a similar market to AIM in Tokyo.

group, and broadening the scope of businesses permitted to banking and insurance groups.

- *Better regulation*. The plan seeks to improve the sharing of key principles and enhancing dialogue with industry actors as well as striving to enhance transparency and predictability of regulation and supervision.
- *Improving the broader environment surrounding the markets*. This would lead to developing and accumulating internationally competitive human resources in the areas of finance, law and accounting, as well as enhancing urban infrastructure as befits an international financial centre.

9. Conclusions: Bolder Steps?

Tokyo has to deliver a solution to Japan's imbalance in asset demand and supply. There may be ample savings in Japan but risk aversion implies that most of these remain in bank deposits, a preference that is unlikely to change significantly given the experience of the global crisis of 2008–09. To resolve this dilemma, Tokyo has to engage actively as an international financial centre, encouraging and supporting its leading financial institutions in expanding abroad as well as being attractive as a destination for foreign investors and institutions. The global crisis may have made the job of intermediation even more difficult but it has also highlighted how important it is for Tokyo to boost its status and influence in global financial markets.

In terms of specific financial markets, the key findings in this report can be summarized as follows.

- There is a risk of over-reliance on the stock market. The world's second largest market continues to provide crucial support for Tokyo as a financial centre and for corporate fundraising; however, this may encourage over-reliance on just one aspect of capital markets and financial services. This is especially important as Japan's strong position in global equity markets will gradually be eroded in the future owing to the economy's weak long-run growth trends as well as competition across Asian equity markets.
- Japan needs to to boost foreign participation in other markets besides equities and reinvigorate the big Japanese bond market, which is currently unique in Asia. This effort could be helped in the short run by the impact of the global crisis on US and EU interest rates and by international investors searching for 'safe haven' currencies and government-backed securities. Although the present, very low level of global interest rates may be unsustainable and is a reaction to the depth of the cyclical downturn, the market trend has been towards lower yields and a flatter yield curve, making Japanese bonds more attractive. The yen is also an important international currency and Tokyo could further promote its use in central bank FX reserves and portfolio management. As capital outflows have waned over the last year, the yen has strengthened, improving investor confidence in the money and bond markets.
- There is considerable potential to achieve greater strategic advantage and visibility from Japanese investments abroad. More focused and longer-term strategies for foreign-asset management would help improve Tokyo's image and influence in the financial services sector and might also help reduce yen volatility.
- The strategy for managing foreign assets may also include expansion of Japanese banks and other financial institutions abroad, especially into markets that offer a higher 'nominal' environment than low-inflation Japan. Foreign investments might include acquisitions, given currently low asset prices and opportunities to rapidly expand business and visibility. This expansion might follow the path taken by other global retail banks, for example. It could also be compared with the successful globalization of Japan's leading manufacturing companies, which used previous cyclical downturns to successfully expand abroad and benefit from recovery.

In terms of the policy background and government targets, these are very supportive of Tokyo as a financial centre and of Japan's financial markets and sector in general. For example, the rapid policy changes promoted by the JFSA with regard to the regulatory and operating environment for financial services are in the direction suggested by market participants and have achieved some success in improving Tokyo's standing as a financial centre (Tokyo's ranking in the last City of London survey rose, for example). This market-friendly attitude ought to help the government achieve its stated specific objectives in terms of improving access to capital markets for companies and also raising the quality of skilled professionals in the financial sector (a problem also highlighted by both the JFSA and market surveys).

International challenges

Tokyo's status and influence as an international financial centre need to be enhanced in ways that are consistent with the specific aims and requirements of the Japanese government and corporate sector in terms of achieving investment and growth both at home and abroad. Tokyo's financial institutions and services need to be global in reach not only to directly support the global operations of the corporate sector (their current, traditional role), but also to support their own future growth and profitability and to achieve the intermediation that Japan needs to resolve its asset demand-and-supply imbalance.

'The challenge for Japan is both to adequately supply capital for its companies and to mobilize and manage an investor base that is extremely risk-averse'

It is likely that Asia will ultimately see the establishment of a global financial centre competing more precisely with London and New York, which lead and innovate in serving global needs for financial services and products. The sheer size of Asian economies and markets will almost certainly create such a dominant competitor to the two leading centres, ultimately with the skills and scope to make an impact at the global level and to bring new ideas and products to markets. But does Tokyo need to compete for this role given its structure of savings and companies? Would it be helpful in achieving targets for the economy, or act as a distraction?

First, Japan has a clear strength and interest in leading-edge manufacturing – and Asia is and will remain the dominant region in this sector. The main questions are how this will be spread across the countries in the region, how countries might specialize, where they will be headquartered, and how they will be financed. If Japan's companies are to continue playing a lead role in global manufacturing and trade, they need to have the backing and encouragement of the government, including a suitable environment for undertaking headquarters, R&D and financial functions and access to fundraising in capital markets. They will need a capable international financial sector in Tokyo.

There are other reasons why Japan must strive to maintain a high-quality financial services industry. In part these are related to its substantial wealth and the need to better manage this wealth, but Japan also needs to be able to understand, and integrate into, global financial markets and trends. In 'knowledge-based' economies, financial-sector knowledge is as important as other technical skills. A country as large as Japan cannot abdicate this responsibility – although it does not need to seek an all-embracing solution via its own financial markets.

The challenge for Japan is both to adequately supply capital for its companies and to mobilize and manage an investor base that is extremely risk-averse. The solution may well require hard work for Tokyo to become fully integrated in international financial markets and services and ensure the appropriate inflows and outflows of capital to rebalance asset supply and demand. Tokyo's financial institutions have to become more, not less, important in the international financial system. This is true of the banks, the stock exchange and other financial services companies.

Whether or not Tokyo becomes a true global financial centre, there are some very strong incentives for it to pursue a leading role as an active international financial centre, expanding the scope and influence of its operations beyond the current sphere.